THE CENTER

FOR ENTREPRENEURSHIP & SMALL BUSINESS MANAGEMENT

Presented to the Libraries
of Kansas

In Honor of a Pioneer
Banking Family

THE CHANDLERS OF KANSAS

COLLEGE OF BUSINESS ADMINISTRATION · WICHITA STATE UNIVERSITY

WSU
BUSINESS HERITAGE
SERIES

WSU
─── ⊒ BUSINESS HERITAGE ⊑ ───
SERIES

The Center for Entrepreneurship
Advisory Board, 1983

Fred Berry
Wichita

Larry Fleming
Wichita

Richard Boushka
Wichita

Fran D. Jabara, Director
Center for Entrepreneurship

Frank Carney
Wichita

Lawrence Jones
Wichita

Ron Christy, Associate Director
Center for Entrepreneurship

Norman Klein
Denver, Colorado

Jamie Coulter
Wichita

Dean Ritchie
Wichita

Martin K. Eby, Jr.
Wichita

Douglas Sharp, Dean
College of Business

Don Slawson
Wichita

THE CHANDLERS OF KANSAS

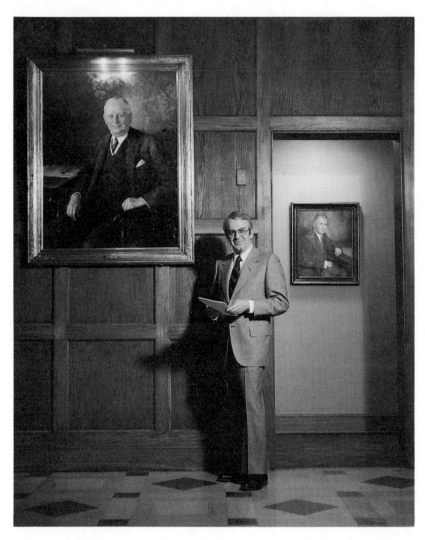

The Chandlers of the First National Bank in Wichita: C.Q. II (1864-1943); C.Q. III (1926-   ); C.J. (1902-1974).

THE
CHANDLERS OF
KANSAS
A BANKING FAMILY

by
Billy M. Jones

Billy M. Jones, Series Editor

Center for Entrepreneurship
College of Business Administration
Wichita State University

ABOUT THE AUTHOR

Billy M. Jones is an endowed professor in the College of Business Aministration at Wichita State University, holding the Chair in Entrepreneurship in WSU's Center for Entrepreneurship and Small Business Management. He also serves as the general editor of the Business Heritage Series, and is the author of many books, including *J.A. Mull: Independent Oilman* and *Dane Gray Hansen: Titan of Northwest Kansas*.

Manufactured in the United States of America.

ISBN: 0-86546-048-5

INTRODUCTION

Charles Quarles Chandler II was 60 years of age when he embarked upon a serious study into his heritage. Like most men, he had heard his parents and relatives speak about "the good old days when men were men and women were women"—when pioneering families lived in an age of excitement, challenge, and heroic achievement on the frontiers of a new nation which was expanding westward into strange and oftentimes perilous environments. The Chandlers had been participants in that migration, and the tales of their sacrifices were vivid in C.Q.'s mind. But, he feared that his progeny might never know the richness of their heritage unless he compiled as complete a documentary as was then available to him, given the all-too-rapid disappearance of the members of the generation which had preceded him. The records he collected are remarkable; so also are the achievements in his own life.

Born in 1864 in Rocheport, Missouri, Chandler was but two generations removed from the time in 1836 when his grandparents left Virginia to settle on the Missouri frontier. He, too, was a pioneer in 1883 when he moved, at the age of 18, to a small agricultural service center at Elk City, Kansas, to start his career as a banker. The rest of his story is a part of the prologue which characterizes the American West. He adapted as his environment changed. Leaving Elk City, he moved first to Medicine Lodge where he grew in stature until his peers chose him, at the turn of the century, as president of the Kansas Bankers Association. By then, he was convinced that Wichita was the emerging financial center in the mid-continent region, and in 1900, he bought the Kansas National Bank and subsequently changed its name to the First National Bank in Wichita—the oldest Wichita bank in continuous existence.

Few men have enjoyed the successes Charles Quarles Chandler II realized after he became a Wichitan—as a banker, miller, and insurance company director. When he died in 1943, it was said that he was one of the wealthiest men in Kansas, but his legacy was more than an amassed fortune. In addition to his bank, which now is the second largest in Kansas, he left a family of bankers who currently operate banks of their own and whose influence spreads throughout the state.

This is the story of that banking family and its progenitor, Charles Quarles Chandler II. His family is highly respected for its strength of character and its consistent professional contributions to the social, civic, and business organizations in Wichita and Kansas. "The Chandlers of Kansas," one prominent Wichitan has said, "are a quality group of men and women—a genuine testimonial to C.Q.'s patient molding, and easily the most significant of his numerous achievements."

Mrs. Emily F. Thayer, Chandler's mother-in-law, wrote him in 1924 in response to his request for genealogical data:

> You know a family is like a tree. First, a single seed is sprouted. It develops some branches and all grow fast, and in course of time, we have a tall and wonderful tree.

To Charles Quarles Chandler II, a person with strong Baptist convictions, her message was meaningful because it bore a special biblical analogy: man plants; the heavens water; and God "giveth the increase." It was the essence of his faith—and the model by which he had built, in the course of time, his "tall and wonderful tree."

AUTHOR'S ACKNOWLEDGEMENTS

Writing a family biography requires the cooperation of numerous individuals, especially in this case, from those who are the most direct, living descendants of a family which had its moorings in the earliest of colonial times. Without exception, the author experienced a totally unselfish and enthusiastic attitude from each of the senior C.Q. Chandler's surviving children. Interviews of exceptional quality were obtained from Elizabeth Chandler Clogston of Ottawa; Olive Chandler Clift of Whittier, California; George Throckmorton Chandler of Pratt; and Anderson Woods Chandler of Topeka—four of the seven children born between 1901 and 1926. Moreover, each of them supplied materials, long stored but not forgotten, from which the accuracy of their recollections and interpretations could be verified.

The same compliments and heartfelt gratitude must be expressed to two of "the Chandler women": Alice Cromwell (Mrs. C.J.) Chandler and Georgia Johnson (Mrs. C.Q. III) Chandler, each of whom made valuable observations about the course of family development from the female point of view and from the vantage of different generations. Their modesty cannot obscure the immense value of their contributions to the successes which the family has enjoyed through the years.

Another rare interviewee was Paul Woods, a man of wisdom and long experience at the First National Bank. His active participation in the bank extended well over three decades, and his direct knowledge of the family spans all of the generations, beginning with C.Q. II. His most impressive contribution (there were many) was a balanced and supportive perspective about the men and their institution—the First National Bank in Wichita—and the changes in policies which, in some cases, came slowly and painfully—but inevitably and surely.

Other perceptive overviews also were provided by the late Gordon Evans, a man who loved his city and labored for it in a variety of important activities during the years which paralleled those of his close friend, C.J. Chandler; by Dale Critzer who shared his knowledge of the Chandlers and the First National from the perception of a respectful competitor; and by Charles Quarles Chandler IV who supplied interpretations from the refreshing viewpoint of one who welcomes the challenges which face the emerging (and fourth) generation of leaders of the First National.

But as Solomon wrote in his wisdom, "The end is better than the beginning of a thing." The author's greatest thanks go alike to two Charles Quarles Chandlers, one living, one deceased. Without the elaborate documentary compiled on the Chandlers in America by C.Q. II, this biography might have been years in the drafting. And without the intelligent guidance and infinite patience of C.Q. III, especially in accommodating the author's irregular schedule by arranging appropriate interview sessions, the enthusiasm to complete the task might have waned to the point of procrastination and default.

Also, two fine student assistants, Mrs. Tammy Smith and Mrs. Connie Jennings, should know of my appreciation for their loyalty and assistance in preparing materials for finalizing this manuscript.

Finally, the author wishes to word a special dedication of his efforts to Russell Anderson Jones, a beloved son who now is a senior medical student at the University of Tennessee Center for the Health Sciences and who has been, like C.Q. II, George, and C.Q. III, his family's mirror into its past through a persistent interest in studying the Jones-Hudson family trees.

Wichita, Kansas   Billy M. Jones
January, 1983

CONTENTS

ILLUSTRATIONS

THE CHANDLERS OF KANSAS

1

A BADGE OF HONOR

On September 16, 1836, Leroy and Sarah Ann Quarles Chandler left Green Springs Valley, Louisa County, Virginia, for the land of Missouri. It was difficult to leave their ancestral home, harder still to uproot eleven children for a trek across the Appalachians to lands about which they knew very little. But the frontier had beckoned, as it would for countless other Americans in the age of westward expansion. For Leroy and Sarah, it was to be a new beginning.

As they traveled, Sarah kept a diary in which she recorded daily observations of both countryside and people. The initial entry, written on the first evening during a drenching downpour, subtly mirrored her apprehensions: "I hope the ultimate turn of this adventure will be more propitious than the commencement." Thereafter she masked her frustrations in cultured rhetoric, even when her experiences contrasted sharply (as they frequently did) with those of a proud Old Dominion upbringing.[1]

It was an arduous journey through wilderness and partially developed lands, along roads which were poorly marked and often impassable. The weather ranged from freezing cold to stifling hot. Rains soaked their clothing and bedding, forcing them at times to spend extra days in camp sunning and ironing in order to "dry out," but they moved relentlessly and confidently through parts of Tennessee, Kentucky, Indiana, and Illinois—a total of 925 miles—before crossing the Mississippi River on November 7 at St. Louis. It had been an act of faith and hope, and a test of courage and perserverance.

The diary ended on November 8 but the family proceeded another 147 miles to Cooper County, Missouri, to a point about ten miles west of Boonville where land was purchased and a new home built. They called it Belle Monte, giving it the name of their ancestral home in Virginia. Ties with their illustrious heritage were too precious to forget, but Leroy and Sarah had embarked on a pioneering venture which would lead to new accomplishments and a further enhancement of the family's name and heritage.

Thus, the year 1836 unquestionably was pivotal in Chandler history. Some truly significant accomplishments lay ahead. But, many outstanding goals already had been achieved. Over two hundred years earlier, Richard, a kinsman, became the first of the Chandlers to chart a course of westward immigration. Sometime after 1620, he sailed from Essex, England, to America in the employ of the Honorable Company of Virginia, fully intending to become a permanent settler. After surviving early depravities and environmental hardships, he eventually laid claim to lands near the present boundary between Virginia and Maryland. His courageous New World venture, important though it would be for the future of the Chandlers in America, nonetheless ended in personal tragedy.[2]

Unfortunately he was "massacred by the treachery of the savages in Virginia" on March 22, 1622, but the following year, three of his four sons (John, Thomas, and Authur) sailed from England on separate ships (to minimize the dangers of shipwreck) to reestablish a claim to Richard's property. George, the fourth son, also joined his brothers in 1635. Eventually all became members of the landed gentry, and in time the Chandler name, through the lineage of Richard and his sons, became as prominent in colonial Virginia as it had been in England.

The Chandlers have deep English roots. Although the origin of the name is lost in antiquity, most authorities agree that it derives from the profession in which its earliest bearers engaged. It is taken from the word candler, meaning "a candle maker." The earliest records list various spellings—Chaundeler, Chandeler, Chanler, Chandlere—but the most frequent is Chandler. Some genealogists assert that men of that name were among the Norman knights who accompanied William the Conqueror to England in 1066.[3]

Others note that through marriage, the Chandlers were related to early Scottish and English kings as well as to other noble families with names such as Cospatrick (Earl of Dunbar), de Curwen (Lord of Workington), and Cleburne (Lord of Cleburne Hall). It is obvious that Richard, the first Chandler in America, was a man of

The family crest, of early English origin.

good breeding and refinement, and his adventurous spirit was characteristic of many men in the age of colonization—evidenced by his sons' decision to follow in his footsteps.[4]

Richard's line of descendants in America remains uninterrupted well into the last quarter of the twentieth century. Through his progeny the Chandler heritage repeatedly has been enriched by marriage to members of other distinguished families and by notable successes in many professional fields—especially after Leroy and Sarah carried the family name into the land of opportunity— to the Great American West. Ultimately Wichita, Kansas, became "home base" for the Chandlers in the West, due largely to the leadership of a pioneer banker, Charles Quarles Chandler II (1864-1943), Richards' grandson eight times removed. That direct and unbroken lineage, notwithstanding other important children born to each entry, extends through succeeding family heads as follows:[5]

CHANDLER	BORN	BIRTH/ RESIDENCE	MARRIAGE(S)
Richard	1577	England/Virginia	_____.
John	1599	England/Virginia	Elizabeth _____.
Richard	1624	Virginia	Mary Fowke
Robert	1659	Virginia	Elizabeth _____.
Robert II	1688	Virginia	Mary Woolfolk
Richard Woolfolk	1729	Virginia	(1) Sarah Thomkins (2) _____Wortham
Timothy	1761	Virginia	Lucy Temple
Leroy	1795	Virginia/Missouri	(1) Eloisa Copeland (2) Sarah Ann Quarles
Charles Quarles	1826	Virginia/Missouri	Anne Elizabeth Woods
Charles Quarles II	1864	Missouri/Kansas	(1) Lizzie Hall Wright (2) Olive Frances Thayer (3) Alice Throckmorton
Charles Jerome	1902	Kansas	Alice Cromwell

Records of the earliest Chandlers (hereafter for convenience the members of the Kansas branch are shown initially in bold letters) are limited to a few notations in official data relating essentially to marriages and land transactions in the counties of Elizabeth City, Henrico, Kent, Hanover, Powhattan, and Caroline. There are, however, isolated annotations in various documents which provide interesting vignettes of their lives and times. Theirs is an interesting history.[6]

JOHN Chandler arrived in Virginia on February 16, 1623, and acquired 1000 acres in Elizabeth City County, lands "bounded on the west by Harris Creek and extending easterly toward Point Comfort Creek and lying on the [Chesapeake] bay." About 1639 he purchased the lands around present Newport News, and in the same year executed a joint bond, dated February 17, 1639, with Samuel Chandler, a London merchant. John listed his occupation as "planter." He held the rank of Major in the Royalist Army, was an elected member of the Virginia House of Burgesses (1645-47), and served as Justice for Elizabeth City County (1652), significant early achievements which indelibly reflect ability, training, and interest. Three sons were born to John and Elizabeth Chandler: John (1622), RICHARD (1624), and William (1625). One of these sons (John) later served in the House of Burgesses.

About Richard, little is known. He was born in Elizabeth City County and married Mary Fowke, daughter of Colonel Gerard Fowke of the Royalist Army who came to Virginia in 1650. On August 3, 1650, he signed, along with other merchants and plantation owners, a petition "to His Highness' Private Council," asking for strict enforcement of laws which would suppress "the planting of English tobacco." Richard and Mary owned a plantation at Varnia, Henrico County, and they had four sons: Richard (1654), John (1656), ROBERT (1659), and Gerard (1660).

Of their childred, Robert continued the branch of the family tree which would become identified as the Kansas Chandlers. Surprisingly few records survive to tell about Robert and Elizabeth Chandler or their large family. Apparently eleven children were born to the union, three daughters and eight sons. Their first child, ROBERT II (1688), was born about the time Kent County was being formed, a development which affected Robert because a part of his plantation was located in the new jurisdiction and had to be resurveyed. Thus young Robert II grew up in what came to be known as St. Peter's Parish in Kent County, Virginia. He later married Mary Woolfolk, and ultimately became the owner of 157 acres of prime land in St. Margaret's Parish in Caroline County.[7] Of the several children born to Robert II and Mary, RICHARD WOOL-FOLK (1729) was fated to extend the branch of the family that would settle one day in Kansas.

Considerably more is known about Richard Woolfolk Chandler. Born on September 15, 1729, at Broomfield in Caroline County, Virginia, he became a millwright (one who is skilled in planning and building mills and maintaining mill equipment), and was married in 1750 to Sarah Thompkins of Hanover County. The marriage united the Chandlers with an important Boonville family which was widely respected for its intellect. Sarah's uncle, Judge Benjamin Thompkins, was a prominent lawyer and circuit court judge, and a man of great prestige and influence.

Richard Woolfolk Chandler also was a deeply religious Presbyterian and proudly wore the title of Reverend for a portion of his adult life. He was twice married, first to Sarah Thompkins who bore him three children: Jane (1759), TIMOTHY (1761), and Richard (1763). After her death, Richard married a Miss Wortham of Caroline County, and the couple had three additional children: (Samuel, Margaret, and John), but records of the second family are incomplete. Richard Woolfolk died in 1774 and was buried at Broomfield in Caroline County.[8]

At the time, the Common Law of England still governed inheritances in Virginia. A prominent feature of the code was the law of primogeniture— which decreed that the eldest son received title to all the landed estate of a deceased father, to the exclusion of all other sons and daughters. The law partially explains the reason why frontier lands in colonial Virginia persistently were claimed and developed.

When the Reverend Richard Woolfolk Chandler died, Timothy became sole heir to his father's property, but he had inherited much more than his material wealth. His father had instilled in him an appreciation for culture and good taste in all matters of personal behavior, as well as a rigid sense of responsibility which had as its cornerstones a deep love for family and heritage, a respect for justice and fairplay, and an insistence upon honesty and integrity as guides for one's decisions.

Timothy wore those traits like a badge "with a rigid sense of honor," as have most Chandlers before and after him. At no time in Chandler history were those cultured characteristics more in evidence than when Richard Woolfolk's Last Will and Testament was probated. In an act of liberality uncommon for his age, Timothy without hesitation divided the estate, which was rightfully and legally his alone, with his brother Richard and his sister Jane. Some things in life are more valuable than material wealth.[9]

A few years later, Timothy joined a Virginia regiment and fought in the Revolution again England. He was present at Yorktown in 1783 when Lord Cornwallis surrendered, and then returned to his paternal estate near Bowling Green, Virginia. In 1788 he married Lucy Temple, daughter of a Revolutionary War hero, Colonel Samuel Temple of Chesterfield County. He settled down to the life of a gentleman farmer, and raised a family of one daughter and five sons, the second son being LEROY (1795). Timothy died in 1825.

For a time, Leroy seemed content to live in Virginia. In 1817 he married Eloisa Copeland, and the couple had three children before Eloisa became ill and died in 1824. The following year, Leroy took Sarah Ann Quarles of Louisa County as his second wife, a union which would be blessed by the birth of 15 children. It would be blessed in other ways.[10]

The marriage of Leroy and Sarah merged the Chandlers with another important and successful Virginia family. The Quarles not only had become prosperous, slave owning planters but also had made notable marks in medicine and the ministry. Moreover, through marriage they were united with other distinguished family names which had impressive ties in both England and the early colonies. Foremost among those names were the Mills, whose ancestry was rooted in English nobility, and the Byrds, prominent colonial Virginians with equally impressive ties to the British gentry.[11]

Sarah Ann Quarles was born on April 20, 1804, at Belle Monte in Louisa County, the plantation home of her parents, Charles and Ann Mills Quarles. Belle Monte was a lovely white, two-story colonial home with a front portico supported by four slender columns. An avenue of cedars, stretching for half a mile, led up to the tastefully landscaped residence which ultimately was enlarged to con-

Leroy Chandler brought his family to Missouri in 1836.

tain 20 bedrooms. The several hundred acres which surrounded the house were divided into farming and pasture lands.

Sarah Ann was the second of ten children born to her parents, and she was only 14 when her father died in 1818 following a brief illness. Thereafter her mother managed, with the help of other family members, to carry on the farming operations and to provide a stable environment for the children.

Sarah Ann Quarles Chandler kept a diary of their trek across Tennessee, Kentucky, Indiana, and Illinois to Missouri.

When Sarah married Leroy Chandler on April 21, 1825, (one day after she had reached majority), the couple made their residence at Belle Monte until their expanding family, which included Leroy's three daughters by a previous marriage, began to place a burden on the plantation's ability to accommodate everyone who lived there. By May of 1836, Sarah had given birth to five daugh-

Belle Monte, Sarah's ancestral home, in Louisa County, Virginia.

ters and four sons: CHARLES QUARLES (1826), Timothy (1827), Eloisa (1828), Margaret (1830), Mary Lewis (1831), twins John and James (1832), Sarah Anna (1835), and Mary Louisa (1836).[12]

After considering all available options, Leroy and Sarah made the decision to seek newer and greener pastures. After 200 years of settlement, most of the farming lands in Virginia were occupied, making it unlikely that they could duplicate previous family successes in the state, and the glowing reports of cheap and abundant lands in the West strengthened their resolve to seek greater opportunities for themselves and their children. Thus, with eleven of their children (nine of whom were under 10 years of age), Leroy and Sarah departed for Missouri on September 16, 1836, knowing that their journey would be long and difficult.[13]

"What a mother!" a relative once wrote reflectively about Sarah's act of faith, or test of courage—or both. Even with the help of some "wonderful Black Mammies who were no doubt her assistants," the writer concluded, it nonetheless was a challenge of major propor-

A sketch of the route followed by the Leroy Chandler family during its move from Virginia to Cooper County, Missouri.

tions to attend to so many children under such conditions. "She has a place all her own in my heart, ... I am proud of her as a Quarles woman."[14]

Leroy showed no less courage. Placing household goods and 12 slaves in wagons and his wife and children in a closed carriage, he started southwestward toward Tennessee, hardly knowing more than mere heresay about what lay ahead of them. He managed their wagon train with skill through the Virginia countryside, reaching and crossing the Blue Ridge Mountains on September 19 and 20 despite uncooperative weather at times.[15]

Sarah's diary tells of the long days of travel, and the short, restless evenings "At night all is commotion fixing the tents, cooking, etc.," she wrote, "and then in the morning taking them up, eating and preparing to go." She described the meadows of western Virginia as the most lovely she had ever seen, but she was less complimentary about the residents. "You scarcely pass a house," she recorded on September 21, "but some dirty barefooted woman will poke out her sunburnt uncombed head to gaze at you—sure mark of ill breeding." Still, the same people were generous to a fault, oftentimes selling the Chandler party needed provisions at ridiculously low prices, and sometimes even giving them milk for the children.

For over a month, their journey was anything but westward. They traveled first to Tennessee which they entered on October 3. Passing through northeastern Tennessee, the caravan turned northward, following the roads in central Kentucky to Frankfurt and Louisville, and reached Indiana on October 19 by crossing the Ohio River at night aboard a steamer. Finally, they turned westward, reaching Vincennes ten days later and eventually crossing the Mississippi on November 7. They remained remarkably healthy throughout the lengthy trip despite almost constant exposure to inclement weather. Only once did they face near tragedy when their carriage driver was bounced from his seat while crossing a rough spot in the road. The horses bolted uncontrollably and wrecked the carriage which contained Sarah and 10 of the children. Miraculously, no one was hurt.

The trip was a series of eye-opening experiences for Sarah; the contrasts betwen Virginia and the western states were severe. "I never witnessed anywhere such total depravity and utter degredation as in Tennessee and Kentucky," she wrote in one place, and in another, "I have a horrid aversion to Indiana ... the people here seem to be in the most abject and degraded state and frequently their situation [is] nothing like as comfortable as ours." In Illinois she wrote, "The people in this country are irreconcilably filthy and a Virginian could scarcely exist amongst them." Finally in Missouri she expressed relief at having reached "this goodly land," adding: "Oh, how pleasant to think after all our journeyings we may still find a home in the very name of which ten thousand charms are concentrated."[16]

She was not to be disappointed. Leroy wasted little time in finding a suitable tract of land in Cooper County, located about 14 miles from the pioneer city of Boonville and five miles from Rocheport on the Missouri River—a spot not far from the center of the state where Nature proved again her skills as a master artist. Nestled on the edge of the great Ozark plateau and refreshed by the Petite Saline Creek which winds its way to the bottoms below, the region Leroy chose was a mosaic of wooded hills and valleys. In selecting a building site, he set the foundations of his new home to capture the beauty of a broad valley which stretched northward for miles. On every side lay virgin forests.[17]

The house he built at first was much more modest than the one he and Sarah had left in Virginia, but they could not resist calling it Belle Monte in honor of her parent's estate. In time, it would become one of the outstanding rural homes in central Missouri. With his slaves, Leroy set about clearing and improving his farmlands, and developing a small orchard. He was a splendid farmer,

The "new" Belle Monte near Rocheport, Missouri.

but he was aware that his managerial style was somewhat lax—for which he compensated by working longer hours. Because of this trait, some thought him to be somewhat aloof to his children, but Leroy merely was using his strengths to meet the basic needs of his family. Already there was a large one to sustain, and over the ensuing decade Sarah would present him with six more children: Isabella (1837), Susan (1838), Eliza (1840), Florence (1841), Robert (1845), and Kelly (1848).[18]

Of Leroy's 18 children, 16 reached maturity. Isabella died in infancy, Robert in 1873 in Dennison, Texas. One of them, Margaret, did not move with the family to Missouri, electing instead to remain with her Uncle Charles Quarles in Virginia where she later married and made her home. The other 15 who survived also married and raised families, providing a powerful multiplier effect in spreading, through their children, the heritage and legacy of their parentage.[19]

Leroy and Sarah were good parents because they had been raised by good parents who placed great importance upon cultured behavior and pride in family traditions. Upon arriving in Missouri, they discovered that social customs were unpolished and often crude, and that business methods were primitive and sometimes devoid of ethics. They always insisted that the Chandler name be worn proudly and that the children hold themselves "steadfastly above the denizens" in the locality. Despite their lack of culture, rustic Missourians nonetheless were fine people—simple perhaps in tastes but extremely kind, sympathetic, and unselfish in offering neighborly assistance. Leroy and Sarah quickly grew to love and appreciate them, and in return received their genuine respect, although a few people in the community thought the Chandler demeanor to be somewhat aristocratic.

The Chandlers did place great store in their Virginia birth and parentage, but those antecedents were a part of that badge of honor which they could no more hide than they could their English heritage. Traditions long developed are indelibly etched into the hearts and attitudes of those who observe them, but the older traditions become, the more maturely and unobtrusively they are exercised, especially when influenced and modified by changes in environment.

Leroy was more affected by the move to Missouri than Sarah, but he continued to enjoy the "congenial society of old times and a good dinner." Moreover, whenever the slavery question was raised, he remained strongly pro-south and an ardent secessionist "by reason of southern kindred and affiliation." However, he became addicted to the friendly, uncomplicated lifestyle in Cooper County, and he loved nothing more than to ride an old sluggish bay mare over to the mill and general store "to meet his rural, simple neighbors and while away an afternoon," especially after the community made him a Justice of the Peace, a post he held for many years.[20]

Sarah remained a true colonial dame, holding most dear the ideals of southern womanhood taught her by her mother. Kelly, her youngest son, remembered her thusly: "Her body was a casket containing the ancestral [markings] of a royal ancestry, and whose scintillations became the brighter by her own actions." Sarah was a gifted woman, and she often attempted unsuccessfully to hide a rich assemblage of talents "in the napkin of modesty," as cultured women of her era felt obliged to do. She had the highest ideals of "maternal and social duty, honor, honesty, justice, and life's miscellaneous responsibilities." She loved her family and was unusually attentive to her married children.

Possessed with intellectual curiousity, she thoroughly enjoyed discussing prophecy with her Baptist ministers, but she also was exceedingly domestic and ungrudgingly shouldered her share of mundane chores, such as tending the poultry, caring for a flower and vegetable garden, and preserving fruit from their small orchard. Sarah was a hospitable hostess and a good neighbor, especially to those from "old Virginia," to whom she often ministered in sickness and distress. She was kind to her slaves and attentive to them when they were ill. Later, she obeyed without hesitation Abraham Lincoln's proclamation which made free men and women of the 41 which the Chandlers owned. Sarah died at Belle Monte on October 26, 1865, Leroy on July 31, 1870.[21]

Together, Sarah and Leroy left their children a legacy not unlike the one they had inherited—a highly principled, God fearing, and responsible sense of social and moral consciousness. They encouraged them to achieve their highest aspirations within that framework of family ideals and traditions. Often they did so at considerable personal and emotional sacrifice, as when their oldest son, Charles Quarles, expressed an interest in becoming a physician. He was a mere lad of 12 and had lived in Missouri only two years, but his parents made arrangements for him to return to Virginia where he would live with and study medicine under the tutlage of his uncle, Dr. Charles Quarles, after whom he had been named.[22]

Years later Leroy would say in an exultant way that his 12 year old son "got on a stage and went to Virginia," implying that the boy had shown great courage in taking the trip alone. No information survives about the journey other than that young C.Q. arrived presumably in the late summer of 1838 and took residence at Inglewood, the plantation home of Dr. Charles Quarles at Gordonville, Virginia. There followed a long and involved program of practical and formal study which included C.Q.'s matriculation in the Medical Department of Hampden Sidney College in Richmond, Virginia, with Uncle Charles serving as his preceptor. Records show that he received his degree in 1848 from the School of Medicine at the University of Pennsylvania. His graduation thesis was on "The Duties of the Physician." Uncle Charles was proud of his nephew's

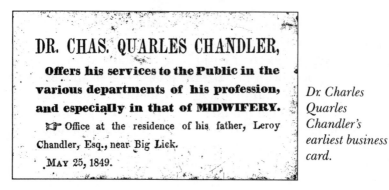

DR. CHAS. QUARLES CHANDLER,

Offers his services to the Public in the various departments of his profession, and especially in that of MIDWIFERY.

☞ Office at the residence of his father, Leroy Chandler, Esq., near Big Lick.

MAY 25, 1849.

Dr. Charles Quarles Chandler's earliest business card.

achievement and wrote Sarah and Leroy: "He will be a credit to all of us."[23]

Soon after his graduation, C.Q. returned to Missouri and located at Belle Monte. One of his first business cards, dated May 25, 1849, is extant and reads: "Dr. Chas. Quarles Chandler, offers his services to the Public in the various departments of his profession, and especially in that of MIDWIFERY." His office was listed "at the residence of his father, Leroy Chandler, Esq., near Big Lick." The location had its conveniences but was not central enough to his practice. He soon moved his office to Connors Mills and remained there until 1853, after which he relocated at Rocheport where he quickly built up a large practice. His transportation was "a large, clay bank colored animal, with large spots on him." He rode the horse, whose name was Mazappa, for many years.[24]

From 1849 to 1861, Charles Quarles Chandler chose to remain a bachelor. He was a busy man with a practice that became increasingly demanding. Not unlike most family practitioners, he pushed his physical endurance beyond reasonable limits, but he was young and thrived on the happy thought that his community depended upon him. He was known for his willingness to go anywhere at any time—day or night—to tend the needs of those who were ill. In time, Dr. Chandler became a stockholder in, and vice president of, the Rocheport Savings Bank. He also found time to be active in his church, especially after he moved to Rocheport. The United Baptist Church of Jesus Christ was without a sanctuary when he arrived in 1853, and he led a drive to construct the congregation's first church building, which finally was completed in 1860.[25]

Through his church activities, he came to know Anne Elizabeth Woods whose grandfather, Reverend Anderson Woods, was one of the earliest pioneer Baptist evangelists in Missouri. As they became better acquainted, they discovered that they shared similar backgrounds and heritages. The Woods name, C.Q. learned, was indelibly linked to English and Irish nobility, and members of the family had come to America long before the Revolution. First settling in Pennsylvania, the Woods eventually migrated to Virginia where Reverend Anderson Woods was born in 1788. Trained as a blacksmith, he started a business in 1807 in Richmond, Kentucky, married Elizabeth Harris in 1808, and became a gentleman farmer two years later. Deeply religious and raised a Presbyterian, he experienced a religious conversion to Baptist teachings and became an itinerant lay minister, ultimately settling in Missouri after 1816. He was ordained in the Baptist Church in 1823, and thereafter organized and served numerous congregations. From 1835 until his death in 1841, he made his home in Paris, Monroe County, Missouri.[26]

It was in that city that C.Q. married Anne Elizabeth on October 10, 1861. James Woods, her father and also the son of Reverend Woods, had died several years earlier, leaving her mother, Martha Jane Stone Woods, to support a family of two sons and three daughters. She was "a splendid type of the women of older times"; she went to work with her needle and not only provided her youngsters with the necessities of a home but also helped each of them attend college. It was a proud and resourceful family into which C.Q. had married. He and Anne made a striking couple and, as is so often said of such relationships, "obviously were made for each other."[27]

C.Q. was the picture of a gentleman of the old Virginia type: handsome, composed, courtly, and always well groomed. "He had a reserve fund of inate dignity," his son once wrote, "which was always on guard [and] could always make people feel his superiority which often created their reverence." Such men, he concluded, "impress the ages with the seal of their chaste and classic individuality. He was one of the last human landmarks of our blessed Colonial Civilization, the memory of which incites us to a higher life."[28]

Dr. Charles Quarles Chandler (1826-1875),
Rocheport physician.

Anne was the essence of a devout Christian wife and woman: attentive, loving, patient, and charitable almost to a fault. "Hers was a beautiful life," one who knew her well has said, "always directed and controlled by the principle of love and obedience to her Heavenly Father." Although she was 12 years younger than C.Q., she was his intellectual equal. She had a strong, positive character, and a mind of masculine strength which was modified and controlled by a woman's gentleness. She was an omnivorous reader—

Anne Elizabeth Woods Chandler (1838-1904).

the Bible, daily newspapers, the best magazines, and books— which she perused carefully and analyzed thoughtfully in order to stay informed about the affairs of the day.[29]

C.Q. and Anne had a congenial and happy marriage based on love for each other and a reverence for God's teachings. Two well loved children, Mattie Lee (1862) and CHARLES QUARLES II (1864), were born to them in the midst of the Civil War, but they managed to hold their family together in security despite the violence and terror often imposed on their community by federal troops

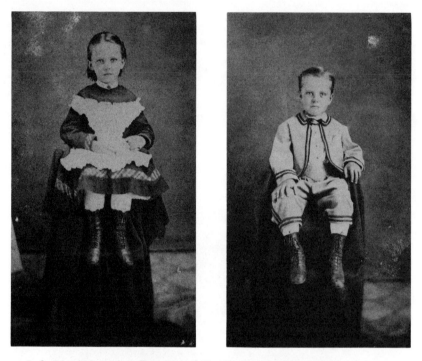

Left: Mattie Lee Chandler, sister of Charles Quarles Chandler II. Right: An Early picture of C.Q. Chandler II, who brought the family name to Kansas.

and bushwhackers. Nor did C.Q. allow his practice to be disrupted, but the confusion made his duties more difficult.

Long hours and physical strain eventually took their toll on the Rocheport physician. In 1874, he suffered a stroke, and his lower limbs were paralyzed. Bathing in warm waters was in vogue for those similarly afflicted, and C.Q. and Anne decided to travel to Hot Springs, Virginia, in the hope that he might be benefitted. Mattie and C.Q. II were lodged temporarily with their Aunt Minerva Berryman at Arcadia in Iron County, Missouri, and they were overjoyed a few weeks later when their parents came to take them home. Unfortunately, the baths were of little help, and C.Q.'s paralysis deepened, eventually affecting the entire spine. He passed away on February 2, 1875, at the age of 49.[30]

"It was a bitter cold night!" C.Q.II later reflected. "I look back now and think of the terrible cloud of sorrow that settled down over my darling mother—how brave she was—for weeks and months she never hummed a tune. Before that she would go singing at her work." It was a tragedy for a mother so young and children so small. Her husband had left them a comfortable home, a small building which was occupied by the Rocheport Bank, and two life insurance policies valued at $2000 and $3000 respectively; however the inheritance hardly was sufficient to allow Anne and the children to live without carefully managing their assets. Anne was a competent household manager but largely was unskilled in business matters; thus, she turned to her brother, Dr. William Stone Woods, for support and guidance. With his love and help, along with some prudent economies and careful planning, the Chandlers were able to live comfortably, if sometimes uneasily, within their limited income.

As so often had been the case, another Chandler family had been forced to call upon the strength of heritage in a time of stress. Anne won the admiration of everyone by the way she assumed the responsibility for raising her young family. She found ways to educate the children despite the fact that Rocheport had no public schools, and she even provided C.Q. II with a year at the University of Missouri. Through it all, Dr. Woods was more than a brother and financial advisor; he became a surrogate father and exerted a powerful influence on young Charles Quarles Chandler.

Years later, when a more mature C.Q. II became seriously interested in tracing the genealogy of his family, he would acknowledge many times the depth of his indebtedness to his uncle whom he revered as one "whose love, help, support and guidance, became a great factor in my own life, and who was one of the very best friends I have had in life." And as he delved into records which sometimes were frustratingly incomplete, he filled the voids by eliciting reminiscences from countless individuals. The stories which had been passed down to him verbally now found substance; he discovered the facts about the rich heritage which was his—and an explanation for the reasons why the Chandler name had become the badge of honor he wore so proudly.

As one publisher friend wrote him: "You were well born, both on your father's and mother's side, and you are keeping up the record in fine style. Blood will tell."[31] But, Charles Quarles Chandler II was one who would have been quick to add to his friend's

A portrait of C.Q. Chandler II at the time of his father's death in 1875.

analysis: "genetics and heritage are extremely important, but it still takes a lot of hard work and faith in the Lord to succeed at anything. Every generation must prove itself worthy of those who have preceded it."

2

THE ROAD TO WICHITA

When his father died in 1875, there was little to suggest that Charles Quarles Chandler II one day would surpass all his ancestors in wealth and prestige. Rocheport, the town of his birth, was little more than a call station for boats on the Missouri River. His father was a country doctor who was left virtually bankrupt by the Civil War. Only through hard work, a few prudent investments, and careful planning were the Chandlers able to recover and live comfortably, if modestly, in their rural setting—at least until Dr. Chandler died.[1]

Still, the Chandlers had a history of being achievers, always arising from their adversities to meet new challenges. Young C.Q. was but ten when he was deprived of his father's influence, but he already had learned much from his teachings and example. Dr. Chandler "was a good, kind, unselfish Christian father" who regularly read the Bible to his family and led them in home worship. C.Q.'s earliest recollections were of "the little Baptist Church in Rocheport" where as a boy he took his turn as a janitor, where his father served as a deacon, and where custom dictated that men sit on one side of the church and women on the other. That church, built through his father's efforts, was an important vestige of his "roots," and when he discovered later in life that it had fallen into "a bad state of repair," C.Q. bore all the costs of renovating the structure and presented it to the city of Rocheport as a community hall and as a memorial to his parents, Dr. Charles Quarles and Ann Elizabeth Chandler.[2]

His father was a man of great dignity whose "superior native capacity" was aided by a classical education, not confined alone to medicine but extending to a strong appreciation for history and literature which he cultivated within an extensive private library. He was active in politics, being a prominent and influential member of the Democratic party. His was a well-rounded and involved life. As W.H. Duncan wrote: "Nature had lavished upon him all the gifts which lead to eminence in his profession and happiness in private life. Burn's law was his: 'where you feel your honor grip, let that still be your border'.... During a period of twenty two years acquaintance with him, personally and professionally, we never saw him activated by a sinister motive, a selfish calculation, or an unbecoming aspiration." Such was the legacy Dr. Charles Q. Chandler left his son.[3]

Life without a husband and father was difficult, but Anne managed as best she could on their limited income. Having been a teacher before she married, she tutored C.Q. and Martha Leeroy (Mattie Lee as she was called) at home until she could afford to enroll them in the Rocheport Academy, a private school taught by L.L. Singleton who had been educated at Kemper Military Academy in Boonville. He ran Rocheport Academy with "the exactness and sterness of a military school," with emphasis upon promptness, punctuality, and precision in academic as well as extracurricular activities. Recitations at public "exhibitions" were expected of all students, and on December 23, 1879, C.Q. dutifully delivered a talk on "Man's Wants" during a special program in the school's auditorium. The discipline "had much influence" on his young mind.[4]

Whatever was missing from the absence of a father was provided by two very influential people in C.Q.'s life: his mother and his Uncle William Woods. Anne was a pillar of stability, always managing her small income "in such a splendid way" that "she was prompt and punctual in all business matters." Even then, principle was first in everything, for her thoughts always were about what was best for her family's reputation. When the Rocheport Bank vacated the small, two story building her husband had bequeathed her, Anne faced a small crisis in that an essential part of her income was now gone. There was little demand for the space, but a Mr. Grossman, who owned the town's only saloon, offered to lease the lower floor and move his business there. Her young son remembered that Anne turned the offer down immediately and emphatically. As much as they needed the income, she nonetheless would not sacrifice principle for revenue. "Is it to be wondered at," C.Q. wrote years later, "that I have always been a prohibitionist and fought the traffic?"[5]

Anne provided her children with a solid intellectual and emotional foundation. She had a well developed mind, always thought through all the important factors of every problem, and openly shared with her children the reasoning behind her decisions. Her Christian faith was a source of great inspiration and comfort to her, and was no less so to C.Q. and Mattie Lee. It was obvious that her "noble, pure, sweet, unselfish life" was one of total dedication to her children's development during their formative years.[6]

She was overjoyed when Mattie Lee married H.J. Hammond, the son of another strong Baptist family, and was proud when C.Q. elected to attend the University of Missouri during the 1881-82 school year. During that year he worked on Saturdays in his Uncle William Woods' Rocheport bank, and took full employment during the following summer. His experiences were such that he "found himself obsessed with a passion for banking," and he elected not to return to the university. Instead C.Q. tried to persuade his uncle to allow him to start a bank at Pilot Grove in Cooper County, but Dr. Woods felt that he was too young at 18 and too inexperienced to assume such a responsibility. He urged patience from his nephew and recommended that he improve his banking skills and knowledge in Rocheport.

Living at home for another year with his mother, whose "influence was the greatest of any person" in his life, strengthened the bonds of respect and companionship between them. Throughout the remainder of her life, Anne would make her home with C.Q. Increasingly however, she entrusted her son's career to her brother, Dr. William S. Woods.

"My Uncle W.S. Woods coming into my life at such an early age," C.Q. confided in his autobiographical notes, "had much to do in shaping my life, especially from a business standpoint. He was a splendid financier and very shrewd and far-seeing. He was of that positive nature like my Mother, knew his ground and stood by his decisions. He was a bold and fearless man, always true to his friends."

Sometime in 1882 Woods moved from Rocheport to Kansas

Dr. William S. Woods, President of the Bank of Commerce in Kansas City, Missouri, and uncle of C.Q. Chandler II.

City to assume the presidency of the Bank of Commerce, and began to look westward for the right opportunity for his impatient nephew. In June of 1883, he invited C.Q. to travel to Kansas and assess the banking opportunities in Elk City and Grenola. Young Chandler was impressed with what he saw and learned in Elk City, so much so that he reported to his uncle his interest in securing part ownership of the Elk City Bank, a private financial institution owned by its president, F.E. Turner.

Elk City, Kansas, in 1883 was an incorporated town of some

700 people in the Louisburgh township of Montgomery County, located approximately 170 miles south and west of Kansas City. It was situated on the Elk River as well as Duck and Salt creeks which furnished power for mills which processed flour, sorghum, and wood. In addition to those products, merchants shipped wheat, corn, and livestock by rail to eastern markets. There were two newspapers, the *Globe* and the *Democrat,* a graded school, and an assortment of churches—Baptist, Presbyterian, Methodist, Episcopal, and Christian. The city was in the heart of a growing agricultural region, and Turner's bank, in the two and one-half years he had owned it, had reached the limit of its resources in servicing the area's needs—"far beyond my most sanguine expectations," he was quoted as saying.[7]

Turner had made inquiries within the banking community, seeking an investing partner to help expand and direct the bank. After what he termed "a long hunt," he extended an offer of full partnership to C.Q. whose purchase of one-half ownership would double the capital of the bank. The agreement was concluded on June 13, 1883, and Turner announced the new partnership with a letter to the editor of the *Elk City Globe,* stating that he had "found it necessary to have an associate and have ... secured Mr. Chas. Q. Chandler as cashier, a young man, but one of several years experience in banking, and of unquestioned integrity, and endorsed by men of high standing." The editor responded by welcoming Chandler and congratulating Turner "upon his acquisition of so pleasant, able, and efficient associate." C.Q., lacking two months of being 19 years of age, had acquired part ownership of the first of many banks he one day would control.[8]

The Elk City Bank was located in the corner of a drugstore which was owned by E.E. Masterman, a young man with whom C.Q. became fast friends. The two businessmen suffered through sluggish economic conditions in 1884, a bad year for many eastern banks, but they both made progress in their social lives when they began courting the Wright sisters. By 1889 Masterman and Chandler would be brothers-in-law, and they would develop a business relationship which would endure for decades.[9]

In 1887 C.Q. purchased Turner's interest in the Elk City Bank and outwardly seemed prepared, after his marriage on October

The Turner and Chandler Bank in frontier Elk City, Kansas, in 1883.

10 to Lizzie Hall Wright, to settle down to the life of a small town banker. His uncle had other plans for his ambitious nephew. In November of 1888 he urged Chandler to move to Medicine Lodge and take charge of the faltering Citizens National Bank in which Woods owned controlling interest. C.Q., Lizzie, and his mother Anne arrived in the city in November; by year's end, Chandler was elected president of the bank.[10]

His task was difficult. The bank had been poorly mananged. Woods and C.Q. changed the charter in 1889 to a state bank, renaming it the Citizens State Bank in an attempt to make it more attractive to the settlers of the area, but the economic conditions in western Kansas made Chandler's business life a struggle. He worked long hours, and slowly restored some of the bank's stability. But, fate dealt unkindly with C.Q. in another way. During the winter months, Lizzie's health failed. For many years a victim of consumption, she found it impossible to adjust to the climate in Medicine Lodge. On July 4, 1889, at the young age of 22 and married less than two years, she succumbed to the insidious disease.[11]

C.Q.'s grief for that "lovely, sweet, noble, unselfish, devoted Christian woman" was severe. He truly loved Medicine Lodge as a place to live and work, but with Lizzie gone he was easily persuaded to accept the cashiership of a newly formed bank in Iowa, the National Bank of Sioux City. From the summer of 1890 until January of 1894, Chandler served Sioux City's "million dollar bank" with such distinction that members of the Iowa community would remember his contributions and pay him high tribute forty years after he had moved on to other challenges.[12]

When the National Bank of Sioux City was merged with the Security National Bank, C.Q. decided to return to Medicine Lodge. He and Uncle William had retained their controlling interest in the Citizens State Bank, and Chandler had not lost his affection for that southwestern Kansas community. After arriving, he found conditions bad again, and he was obliged to take firm control of the bank in order "to straighten it out." Conditions for the First National Bank in Medicine Lodge were deteriorating also, and the Citizens' directors voted to purchase all of the stock in the struggling bank, consolidating on February 28, 1894, the First National with the Citizens State.[13]

Hard times for over a decade had driven "hundreds and thousands" of residents in western Kansas to abandon their farmlands after 1889 when the unassigned Indian lands in the Oklahoma Territory were opened to settlement. Chandler was especially stunned by the population losses in Barber County when the Cherokee Strip became available in 1893, but he was wise enough to recognize the opportunities the phenomenon presented. Property values in the Medicine Lodge area fell dramatically, and C.Q. bought "quite a bit" just for the taxes. Additionally, he knew that many of the new towns in Oklahoma,

C.Q. Chandler II, shortly before his marriage in 1887.

such as Alva and Woodward, largely were made up of former Kansans who soon would need the services of financial institutions. An experienced banker "spread his wings."

In the fall of 1893 with his cousin J.W. Berryman as a partner, C.Q. started a small private bank at Pond Creek, a town located approximately 20 miles north of present Enid, Oklahoma. The following spring, Chandler joined Berryman and W.S. Fallis, another cousin, in opening the Alva State Bank, but soon sold his

Lizzie Hall Wright at the time of her marriage to C.Q. Chandler II. She died of consumption in 1889.

interests in both banks in order to devote his efforts to the Citizens State in Medicine Lodge. Nonetheless, the entrepreneurial bug had bitten him. Over the next three decades he either would start or purchase control of almost three score financial institutions, and during that period he would become one of the wealthiest and most influential men in Kansas.

Significant personal development accompanied his expand-

Olive Frances Thayer who became Mrs C.Q. Chandler II in 1898.

ing business horizons. In the summer of 1895, Chandler met Olive Frances Thayer in the Sunday School at the Baptist Church in Medicine Lodge. Olive was visiting her parents, the E. J. Thayers of Iola, who had come to live on a farm, two miles west of Medicine Lodge, owned by an uncle, Dr. Eli P. Miller. From their first meeting, C.Q. was "taken with her." She was a winsome lass of strong character who impressed C.Q. as "noble, unselfish, [and]

C.Q. Chandler II, President of the Citizens State Bank in Medicine Lodge, Kansas, in 1899.

far-seeing, a devoted, conscientious, practical Christian, consistent in every act of life."

Olive was the daughter of Edmond Joseph and Emily Frances (Benedict) Thayer. The origin of the Thayer name is German, although the first members of that family came to Massachusetts Bay Colony in 1630 from England. The Benedicts, who called

Nottingham, England, their home, migrated in 1638 to New England. Ultimately members of both families removed to Illinois where Edmond and Emily met and married during the Civil War. First Lt. Thayer twice was wounded, resulting in permanent damage to his right leg, but after the war he confidently set out for Kansas in a covered wagon with his young wife where he homesteaded 160 acres of land west of Fort Scott in Bourbon County. Then in 1878 Edmond bought a mill and moved to Iola so that his children could have the advantages of a good school. Olive graduated from Iola High School in 1891 and became a successful teacher.[14]

Misfortune brought Olive and C.Q. together. In the winter of 1893, Edmond's mill burned to the ground, destroying "all we owned in two hours' time." To earn a livelihood, he accepted his Uncle Eli Miller's offer to work on a farm in Barber County, and in the summer of 1894, Edmond moved most of his family there by train. Olive remained in Iola but visited her parents frequently until they returned to Iola in late 1895.

A three year romance, made difficult by the distance which separated them but strengthened by the bond which grew with each treasured visitation, culminated in marriage on June 22, 1898, at Mrs. Thayer's home in Lincoln, Nebraska, where she had moved the previous year following the death of her husband. After a visit to "the exposition in Omaha" and a wedding trip to the west coast, C.Q. and Olive returned to Medicine Lodge where, it was announced, they would make "their home for the immediate future, at least." The marriage was a fortunate step for the maturing banker, for Olive "always stood four square with [him] on everything where principle was at stake."[15]

She supported him in a courageous act shortly after their marriage. In April a referendum had been held in Medicine Lodge to determine if the city should "enforce the prohibition law or allow it to be violated." An element supporting the sale of liquor carried the election and decided to permit a saloon to open on July 4 as a part of a planned Independence Day celebration. The "wets" employed Put Hill, a black man with one leg, to operate the saloon, and arranged with Captain J.A. Stine in Alva, Okla-

The spacious Chandler residence in Medicine Lodge.

homa, for the delivery of a large quantity of beer from a St. Louis brewery.

Thus, on July 4, 1898, the saloon opened to a thriving business; crowds began to swarm up and down the stairs leading to the make-shift, second story pub. Sometime around 10:00 A.M., a disturbed C.Q. Chandler approached the bar, asked to be served, but was refused by a cautious Put Hill who knew and respected the banker's sentiments. Chandler then swore out a warrant, had the beer seized, and Hill was placed in jail. The beer later was destroyed by the sheriff, and Captain Stine, who had not been paid for it, sent his attorney to Medicine Lodge to collect damages under the threat of legal action—"to which threat we gave him a hearty laugh."

A rebuffed Stine, who later entered the banking business in Alva, became Chandler's outspoken enemy. Put Hill, who was deserted by the men who hired him, was unable to pay his fine and served several months in jail. He bore C.Q. no grudge and emerged from confinement with friendship and admiration for him. Pleased also was a proud mother Anne. Her son's action demonstrated again the wisdom of one of her favorite scriptures: "Bring up a child in the way he should go, and he will not depart therefrom."

Conditions caused C.Q. to diverge from one family tradition. His father had been a local leader in the Democratic party even when such affiliation was not popular in post Civil War Missouri, and C.Q. became an ardent supporter of the party. By 1896 however, the Democrats were irrevocably committed to a liberal monetary philosophy based on the free coinage of silver, a position Chandler thought unwise. After studying the issue carefully, he decided that he no longer could support a party which advocated such a policy. He voted for William McKinley, his first ever for a Republican candidate, and the switch in parties thereafter became permanent.

During the early fall preceding the election, he journeyed to New York on business but spent considerable time discussing the national political situation. He became convinced that McKinley would be elected and that the prospects of complete business recovery were foreshadowed. After returning home, he began to buy cattle and sell them to his customers as investments, and by the time McKinley took office in March of 1897, some southwestern Kansans had realized significant profits—and a banker's perception had earned him greater respect.

Improvements in the business climate encouraged expansion. In the spring of 1897 Chandler (along with W.S. Woods, E.E. Masterman, and W.H. Sloan of Independence) started a highly successful, though small bank in Garnett. Called the Bank of Commerce, the new institution had as its officers C.Q. Chandler, president; W.H. Sloan of Independence, vice president; and E.E. Masterson of Elk City, cashier. The following year Chandler successfully outbid a Hutchinson bank to become the depository for Kiowa County funds, a coup for the Citizens State Bank since Kiowa had no bank of its own. C.Q.'s bank already was the depository for Barber County.[16]

The parade continued into southwestern Kansas towns. For many years Chandler had watched the economic development of a region whose principal industry was cattle raising. He had learned the techniques of watching the process of bringing cattle to a marketable state, including the effects of range movement on fattening and weight shrinkage, of the availability of range grasses, and of the status of the market in determining the best time to buy and sell. When conditions were favorable, it was not unusual for him to make huge loans on herds, and in the process he built the Citizens State Bank of Medicine Lodge into "one of the strongest institutions of this portion of the state."[17]

Some bankers in the region were more conservative, but C.Q. defended his practice of making substantial loans to ranchers. "I have loaned money on cattle for fifteen years," he was quoted as saying, "and I consider no security in the West better. It must be conducted judiciously, the same as loaning money on real property. I have made only one bad loan during that time, and then I lost only $75." Victor Murdock wrote years later, "As much as any man alive, Mr. Chandler has observed the cattle tableau of the plains from early days until now ... [and has played] an important part as a big cattle man."[18]

After the Republican victory in 1896, C.Q. was convinced that his portion of the southwest faced a period of phenomenal growth, a belief which had urged him to acquire the other bank holdings during 1897-98. On August 30, 1899, he and Jerome W. Berryman (then cashier of the Elk City Bank) concluded an agreement to purchase the Farmers and Stockgrowers Bank of Ashland in Clark County from George Theis, Jr. It was intended that Berryman would become cashier and run the bank, but responsibilities in Elk City delayed those plans. To bridge the time gap, Chandler brought his cousin, Paul Scott Woods, from Rapid City, South Dakota, as assistant cashier to A.M. Vanlingham who managed the bank until Berryman arrived.[19]

A few months later Chandler and Berryman drove by buggy to Meade, a city without a bank, and they soon opened a small one with a capital of $5000. Farther west was Liberal, county seat of Seward County, which also was without a bank. The banking partners sent Paul Woods from Ashland to visit with local businessmen who had requested that someone come to evaluate the needs of the growing community. Woods asked Ray "Skinney" Millman, editor of the *Liberal News*, if there was a man in the area "with sand in his craw and whose word you can tie to" who might help in organizing a bank. Millman arranged a meeting between Woods and John E. George, a former Texas drover who had become a prominent area rancher. After a short overnight discussion and a hand shake the next morning, an agreement to establish the Liberal State Bank was reached, and the bank was opened on July 2, 1900, with George as a principal investor and Woods as cashier. It was a profitable enterprise and earned, according to Chandler, "about $10,000 on the investment the first year."[20]

As his holdings grew, C.Q.'s reputation expanded throughout the Kansas banking community. His colleagues accorded him a major honor on June 7, 1899, at the state bankers' convention in Abilene, when they elected him to serve as president of the Kansas Bankers' Association for the next year. Earlier that morning he had delivered a paper on "State Funds and What To Do With Them," pointing out the weaknesses in state laws which made only Topeka banks eligible as depositories for state funds. Such funds, he stated, should be placed in those banks offering the highest interest returns, provided stipulated bond security requirements were met. Not everyone agreed with his point of view, but the paper evoked a lively discussion.[21]

Citizens of western Kansas certainly agreed with another of his positions—that the area needed to build a telephone service. An attempt made in early 1900 by the Reese Construction Company had ended in failure, but Chandler was too public minded to let the situation pass. He persuaded the Kansas and Missouri Telephone Company of Kansas City to extend their lines from Harper to Woodward, by way of Attica, Medicine Lodge, Kiowa, and Alva. Then, joining with Waldron Chase, he obtained sufficient subscribers to ensure the construction of a system for Medicine Lodge featuring automatic telephones which spared the expense of maintaining an exchange office and resulted in considerable savings to subscribers. During the week of September 27, 1901, the system became operational.[22]

By 1901, Chandler's banking horizons had broadened even farther with the acquisition of what eventually would prove to be the most important financial institution he would serve—the

Interior of the Kansas National Bank of Wichita at the time C.Q. Chandler purchased it in 1900.

Kansas National Bank in Wichita. C.Q. first learned of its availability in February of 1900 in a letter from Elsberry Martin, a director and cashier of the bank. Martin had written at the request of J.O. Davidson, president of KNB, who had sought unsuccessfully to consolidate his bank with the Fourth National Bank in Wichita. Chandler was known to be searching for a Wichita bank, having attempted to purchase the old Wichita National several years earlier.[23]

A first meeting between Chandler and KNB officials was inconclusive. C.Q. rationalized his indecisiveness in various ways. He was not interested in leaving Medicine Lodge, having been happily settled in the community for some time. Moreover, he was prospering, and his Citizens State Bank was every bit as big if not larger than the Kansas National Bank. Further, he was not sure that he had a person in his organization who was available to run KNB. He first had F.E. Carr examine the situation, but Carr expressed no interest; later he sent E.E. Masterman to consider the opportunity—and found in him a willing partner. After several days of studying and investigating, Chandler made arrangements in early May of 1900 to purchase the Wichita bank and to move Masterman from the Garnett Bank of Commerce to become vice president and chief operations officer of KNB.[24]

The Kansas National Bank became a family affair, both in investments and management. Chandler and Masterman were joined by Dr. W.S. Woods and J.W. Berryman, all of them related to each other, in pledging capital to purchase the stock. The four men became directors, as did C.W. Southworth, C.H. Brooks, and Elsberry Martin. Martin retained his previous role as cashier. C.Q. became president and announced his intentions to divide his time between the Citizens and KNB while continuing to reside in Medicine Lodge.[25]

"The new stockholders," the *Medicine Lodge Cresset* reported on May 11, 1900, "have a string of banks from Kansas City to Carlsbad, New Mexico, and their object in securing a bank at Wichita is to have a central institution convenient for handling the big cattle business of the southwest." Chandler confirmed the analysis, stating that "the cattle business of this section is permanent and is going to be more and more the cattle supply grounds of the United States. I have seen this for years and all that time I have been figuring to get hold of some of these good Wichita banks."[26]

Shortly after the purchase of KNB, Chandler demonstrated just how successful he had been in acquiring southwestern financial institutions. He published and circulated a booklet entitled "A Little Community of Interests, Out in Kansas," which revealed that the Chandler-Woods investment team had bought interests in 18 of the leading banks in the state. An impressed Medicine Lodge newspaper editor referred to Chandler as "the Monte Cristo of Barber County," and predicted that he would not be content until his empire "spans the earth from ocean to ocean, from the lakes to the gulf." And, the editor concluded, aside from his title as the "bank king," Chandler was a splendid good man whose Midas' touch he hoped would continue until he could "send us a sack of shiners [gold coins] to play with."[27]

For five years, C.Q. remained in Medicine Lodge. He gave direction to the Wichita operation through Masterman, thanks

First automobile purchased in Wichita, a 1902 curved-dash Oldsmobile, which served as a commuting vehicle for the rising banker. Shown with C.Q. Chandler II is his oldest daughter, Margaret.

at times to the long distance telephone system he had promoted for the region. He also commuted when he could, but the distance was great, even after he bought the first automobile sold in Wichita. The car, a small one cylinder Oldsmobile which was rated at 40 miles per hour, "excited as much curiousity as a circus parade" when it was delivered in late March of 1902, but required frequent adjustments by an "expert." C.Q. had hoped it would make travel between his various banks easier, but roads were poorly kept and the automobile generally was unreliable.[28]

Still, he made frequent use of the machine. On April 9, 1902, he and J.D. Fair drove from Medicine Lodge to Sharon, a distance of 13 miles. They "clipped off 12 miles per hour ... going like the wind," and made the trip in one hour and nine minutes—establishing a record for that vicinity. Again in May, he and Will Merrill went to Sharon and drove through a small herd of cattle. All but one of the animals fled in fright from "the strange 'cow pony' that came among them." The one steer stubbornly charged the Oldsmobile, ramming it into a barbed wire fence and throwing the occupants onto the ground. "Nobody was hurt," the *Barber County Index* reported, "and the steer walked off with the air of one who had effectively blocked the wheels of progress and discouraged the introduction of new-fangled methods of rounding up cattle."[29]

Chandler's Oldsmobile lost another race. In mid-September, C.Q. and Waldron Chase started for Wichita, intending to make the drive in half a day in order to allow Chase to catch an evening train. Their adventure "spoiled the best part of a day," and when they arrived, "Mr. Chase's train was out and gone." Again the *Index* philosophized charitably: "The auto is a swift vehicle but Kansas roads are a quality which must be figured on."[30]

Increasingly, C.Q. had to figure on more than the status of Kansas highways. He found himself spending most of his work days in Wichita and making the long drive back for weekends in Medicine Lodge, the town he and Olive had regarded as home since their marriage. And, after their children began to arrive—Margaret (1901), Charles Jerome (1902), and William Woods (1904)—it became more difficult to consider relocating, despite the fact that Chandler's other business interests "away from Medicine Lodge" were multiplying. In the first year of operations at the Kansas National Bank, deposits reached $1 million on June 28, 1901, almost double the volume at the time of the bank's purchase on May 4, 1900.[31]

It became more and more burdening "to get in and out of Medicine Lodge," but both C.Q. and Olive endured the frequent separations ungrudgingly until his mother, Anne Elizabeth Woods Chandler, died on August 8, 1904. It was difficult to accept the loss of that sweet, unselfish woman who had made the moves with him to Elk City, Medicine Lodge, Sioux City, and back to Medicine Lodge—and was his constant companion for a quarter of a century, a loving supporter of his wife, and a doting grand-

*Portrait of C.Q.
Chandler II in 1903,
with daughter
Margaret and son
Charles Jerome.*

mother to his children. In time the resolve in both C.Q. and Olive weakened. They yielded to the obvious need to move to Wichita, renting on October 17, 1905, a house at 13th and Fairview as their first home in the new city.

It was a sad time for a southwest Kansas community. "C.Q. Chandler," the *Barber County Index* lamented, "has finally decided to make Wichita his permanent home. His household goods were packed and shipped the first of the week and Mrs. Chandler and the children left yesterday. Medicine Lodge regrets to lose this distinguished and prominent family."[32] However, time would prove again the truth in an oft-quoted addage: one city's loss is another's gain. And after eight generations, one branch of the Chandlers of Virginia, decendants of Richard (1577-1623), had found permanent moorings in Wichita, Kansas.

Anne Woods Chandler, C.Q.'s mother, in later years.

3

THE CHANDLERS BECOME WICHITANS

Between May 4, 1900, and October 17, 1905, Charles Quarles Chandler enacted his own version of Charles Dickens' *Tale of Two Cities*. It was the best of times, for his persistent work in the new Wichita bank was proving highly rewarding. By 1905 deposits had grown to a record $2 million with loans amounting to $1 million. But it was the worst of times, for he was battling stubbornly during that period to retain his home in Medicine Lodge, resulting over time in a fatiguing, communter life-style which increasingly did injustice to both business and family.[1]

Yet, Charles Quarles Chandler was the complete businessman: smart, courageous, indefatigable—and a man of broad vision. Wichita to him already had become his springtime of hope. It was a city of almost 25,000 people which had but three national banks. The Kansas National Bank was the smallest of the three, but C.Q. felt he had a "golden opportunity" to build a solid institution in a city he knew was destined to become the financial center for the region. In the end, there was no other decision, difficult though it was for all of the family to accept. It was time to make a new home in Wichita and allow the city to become the hub of his business interests, which had expanded before he left Medicine Lodge to include substantial ownership in a new Wichita milling operation.[2]

The move in October of 1905 was sad for the Chandlers but certainly not their "winter of despair." They made their adjustments with relative ease. The spacious home they had occupied in Medicine Lodge was replaced with a comfortable rented house in Wichita. At least C.Q. was at home more evenings per week which made for a balanced family regimen. Moreover, their three children—Margaret, Charles Jerome, and William Woods—who were little more than toddlers, were permitted to feel more con-

The Chandler Children in 1906, showing L to R: Billy, Charley, and Margaret holding baby Elizabeth.

sistently the all important influence of both parents. And happily, Olive and C.Q. had lived in their new home less than a year when their fourth and last child, Elizabeth, was born on May 26, 1906.[3]

No doubt her birth played a major role in speeding Chandler's plans to erect a permanent home for his growing family. In July of 1908 he engaged S.G. Bond, a Wichita contractor, to construct a new residence on College Hill which was described as "large and modern and built in colonial style." It was projected "to cost in the neighborhood of $13,000." The home, completed in October of 1910, was registered as 200 South Clifton. It would remain C.Q.'s home until his death in 1943.[4]

The South Clifton residence was a well designed, spacious home with three stories and a basement. It was characteristic of C.Q. to build for permanency and to utilize property to its fullest. The driveway to the home entered off Clifton, passing underneath an overhanging porch room (which served as the master bedroom) and exiting onto Oakland Street. The basement housed a furnace which burned distillate fuel oil, an area for recreational and avocational activities, and yet another section for laundry and ironing services. The main floor was arranged to accommodate everyday living: a drawing room with a gas burning mantel-type fireplace, an adjoining sitting room, a formal dining room and kitchen, a cloak closet, and a staircase leading to the upper floors. Additionally a back porch, attached to the kitchen-butler's pantry area, contained an icebox with an outside service door which permitted daily deliveries by commercial ice trucks.

The second floor contained five bedrooms, four with separate baths. There also was an unheated sleeping porch which the children used in summertime since the house was not air conditioned. A laundry chute connected with the basement and was large enough not only to drop soiled clothes through but also for the children (and later, grandchildren) to climb between floors in their playtime routines. Finally, the third floor was an unfinished, open recreation space except for a maid's room and con-

200 South Clifton, the Chandler home for almost four decades.

necting bath. Outside was a flat porch which also was used for summertime sleeping.[5]

Although not opulent, 200 South Clifton was a showplace for its day, a home of space and comfort befitting the life-style of a rising businessman and his growing clan. The house was designed for family living, and it accommodated the purposes of Olive and C.Q. who sought to mold the character of their children more through wholesome family activities than through lavish social entertainment. In the earlier years, they chose to educate the children at home by providing tutors and adapting a special room for their instruction. Christian values were taught by example and by involvement in regular church attendance.

C.Q. had a strong, almost domineering personality. He was regarded by his family as a wonderful father who inspired love and demanded great respect. His children were in awe of him because his mannerisms left no doubt about his expectations; he gave directions positively and firmly, leaving little to discuss or negotiate. There was a Chandler way of doing things, and all "obeyed the rules," even C.Q. whose habits were the epitome of the devout Christian father. He neither smoked nor drank, and seldom attended functions where intoxicants were served. He was a strict disciplinarian—an attitude in which Olive fully supported him—and expected his children, until the day they married, to observe an eleven o'clock curfew. And, he was very protective in other ways, always insisting that Olive and the girls not "go out on the street alone to shop or anything." In all ways he cared about his family and "was marvelous to them."[6]

Shortly after their move from Medicine Lodge, C.Q. and Olive presented their letter and were united in fellowship with the First Baptist Church in Wichita. C.Q. immediately was appointed to membership on the Finance Committee, and on March 8, 1906, was elected as a deacon. Later his leadership as chairman of the board of deacons would span many years and involve some of the more responsible decisions affecting the work of the church. In time the children would make their confessions of faith and received baptism, uniting the family in ways that only religious worship can.[7]

The Chandlers' happiness and serenity were jolted rudely on July 3, 1912, when Margaret became seriously ill with a poorly understood and terrifying disease—infantile paralysis. Born on September 8, 1901, in Medicine Lodge, eleven-year-old Margaret was bedridden for a month before the full effects of her illness were known. Her left leg was totally paralyzed, and she suffered from acute neuritis. It was crushing blow for one so young, and heart breaking to her parents. A frantic search for local assistance was unproductive, and C.Q. decided to take her to live by the seashore at Asbury Park, New Jersey. He took temporary leave from his banking responsibilities, packed up the entire family, and headed east where he hoped to find specialists for Margaret's afflictions.[8]

In Philadelphia, he was introduced to Dr. Charles K. Mills who successfully dealt with her neuritis. He recommended that she be placed under the care of a Dr. Davis, a splendid orthopoedist, who along with his assistant, Dr. Frank D. Dickinson, established a rehabilitation routine which by November had Margaret walking on crutches. However, it was obvious that her knee needed bracing, and P.W. Hanicke, a fine craftsman who worked for

C.Q. II and his four children in Asbury Park, New Jersey, in 1912, where they had gone to help Margaret recover from her paralysis.

Charles Lentz and Sons Brace Company, was engaged to fashion a metal support for Margaret's knee. Finally, after eight months of treatment, she had made sufficient progress to allow the family to return to Wichita.[9]

The experience had a dramatic impact on C.Q.'s life. "The Lord has been kind," he confided to a friend, "in permitting me to accumulate wealth and in allowing my daughter to recover. I feel now that I owe a distinct debt to Him that I must try to discharge by helping other handicapped children." Since Margaret was required to return periodically to Philadelphia for treatment and observation, Chandler began the practice of taking along other disabled children and paying for their therapy. In all, 28 children were helped in this way, and Chandler bore all their expenses. Ultimately the costs became too excessive for one philanthropist to finance, and many of the children found the long separations from their families too oppressive.[10]

Necessity sparked a humanitarian's sense of innovation. The need for a Wichita clinic was imperative, C.Q. felt, and he pushed

for and finally founded in March of 1915 the Wichita Orthopoedic Clinic managed by Mrs. Alma R. Okeefe, a graduate nurse.
Then during his next trip to Philadelphia, he persuaded P.W.
Hanicke to move to Kansas City as part owner and manager of
the P.W. Hanicke Manufacturing Company which Chandler financed. Additionally, Dr. Frank Dickson expressed interest in
moving his practice to Kansas City if proper hospital connections
could be arranged. To C.Q. it was a grand opportunity.[11]

Chandler knew that the Christian Church Hospital was under
construction in Kansas City, and that J.W. Perry, President of the
National Bank of Commerce and a longtime friend, was Chairman of the Board of Trustees for the hospital. Together, Chandler and Perry developed a plan to build an orthopoedic clinic
on the hospital's roof garden—and to add Dr. Dickson to the staff
as director of all orthopoedic work. By a special arrangement,
Dickson agreed to drive to Wichita once each month and donate
his services to the patients at the Wichita Orthopoedic Clinic.[12]

For a time, C.Q. personally provided the maintenance funds
for the Wichita clinic, including Dr. Dickson's travel expenses,
but the successes enjoyed by the clinic attracted other donors.
Especially instrumental early in raising funds for the work was
John B. House of Wichita whose influence in the Midian Shrine
and Consistory proved quite valuable. Other civic organizations,
such as the Elks and Scottish Rite Masons, also joined the effort.[13]

Increased outside funding broadened Chandler's vision. The
rapid growth in the number of Wichita patients convinced him
that there were hundreds, even thousands, of crippled children
in Kansas yet to be identified who might never find a way to have
their needs met. Only with a uniform program established by
law which would provide state funding could the matter be dealt
with appropriately. A special effort was needed; accordingly, the
first state conference for crippled children was called and held
in Wichita in November of 1925, at which over 300 prominent
Kansans met and organized the Kansas Society for Crippled
Children. Chandler was honored by being unanimously elected
to serve as president of the new organization.

Chandler recruited a few strong, key individuals to help direct
the work of the Society, men such as Harve Plumb of Wellington

and Earle W. Evans of Wichita. Also enlisted were the American Legion, Kiwanis International, Lions International, and the Kansas Federation of Women's Clubs. Evans was wise in the way of legislative activity, and he urged the Society to do its "home work"—to begin a state-wide fact finding program regarding disabled children before launching a campaign to obtain state legislation. A part of their efforts, he advised, should be to conduct an intensive educational program in order to gain public support. Once armed with the facts and supported by popular sentiment, their appeal could prove irresistable.[15]

Under Chandler's supervision, the Society began its progam, aiming its strongest efforts at what was regarded as the main barriers: public lethargy and parental fear. C.Q. traveled widely, arranged free clinics, and made public addresses to countless organizations and assemblages. After two years of such activities, the Society's board fashioned its first legislative appeal for help—asking "for a temporary commission to make a formal survey of the state to find all crippled children, with a full history of each case." The request was approved and funded, and Chandler was appointed chairman of the temporary committee.[16]

A census of over 6000 disabled children was developed and presented in a report to the legislature, along with a proposal that a decentralized program be established in Kansas, giving each of the 105 counties the funds to provide hospitalization, education, and placement of its young cripples. No action was taken in 1929 on the proposal, largely because it became ensnarled in political partisanship when the Republican Party adopted it as a plank in its platform. Hard work, however, ultimately paid off in the spring of 1931 when Democratic Governor Woodring removed the issue from partisanship and recommended the passage of a crippled children's bill. The legislature responded almost unanimously by enacting it into law. Not surprisingly, Charles Quarles Chandler was appointed as chairman of the first permanent commission, to which one newspaper commented: "It was a good appointment, so good it was inevitable."[17]

Every movement of note, it has been said, is born first in a man's heart. Obsessed with compassion for his own daughter's plight, C.Q.'s heart opened to others similarly afflicted and caused him to use his wealth and influence to alleviate the suffering of countless handicapped children in Kansas. To him, it was his Christian duty, a fulfillment of the Puritan concept of the stewardship of wealth. He continued his leadership role in the movement throughout the remainder of his life, and established a foundation to ensure that future generations of disabled Kansas children could receive medical assistance and physical therapy. More than any of his many civic endeavors, his work for the Society for Crippled Children stands as the highest monument erected to his memory.

Throughout Margaret's sudden illness and partial paralysis in 1912, Olive stood solidly behind C.Q. in making the decisions which placed her daughter's welfare above all other family considerations. Closing 200 South Clifton temporarily, as comfortable and secure as the new home made them all feel, was no sacrifice in Olive's mind if Margaret's health and physical condition might be improved by residence on the eastern seacoast. She was constant in her attendance to Margaret's every need, ever present despite the frequent lack of sleep as well as the burden of caring for her younger children who understood imperfectly the severity of their sister's malady.

To her friends in Medicine Lodge and Wichita, Mrs. Chandler was a pillar of strength. Those who knew her well recognized the source of her resolve to nurse Margaret back to stable health, for during her residence in Medicine Lodge Olive had borne and lost three children in infancy. She suffered her grief quietly but never fully recovered from their deaths, evidenced by the fact that when the family moved to Wichita, she had insisted that their bodies be removed and re-interred in the Wichita cemetery. She was determined that there would not be a fourth grave over which to mourn.[18]

Regrettably, there was to be a fourth grave, most untimely and totally unanticipated. Olive herself became ill in July of 1915 and spent ten days in the Wichita Hospital, undergoing what was reported to be "a minor operation." It was much more serious than was first thought, and when she failed to make a satisfactory recovery, C.Q. quietly but immediately took her by train to Chi-

Olive Frances Chandler died in Chicago following surgery in 1915.

cago, entering her in the Presbyterian Hospital where she was examined by a specialist and operated on for a stomach tumor. After her surgery, the surgeons were optimistic and informed

Chandler that "it was not serious" and that they believed "she would recover speedily." However, the shock of the second operation apparently was too much for her, for Mrs. Chandler died suddenly and unexpectedly on August 2, "the result of an inexplicable, unusual condition which sometimes follows an operation."[19]

Thus, a noble life had ended, and she was mourned by both family and community. She was a woman "of a remarkably beautiful character and poise, whose interests lay in her home, her church, and her charities." She essentially was "a home woman," and her devotion was to her children almost to the exclusion of other social enjoyment. Once when asked why she did not attend conventions, Olive responded that there were four reasons—Margaret, Charles, William, and Elizabeth. "She could have engaged servants," one observer noted, "but she knew she could not hire a mother."[20]

Dr. Guy L. Brown, pastor of the First Baptist Church euolgized Mrs. Chandler as a devout Christian woman. "Modest and retiring in disposition, she was an earnest worker, always thoughtful of others rather than of herself." She was "an ardent churchwoman ... her mind, pocketbook, good judgment were always among the first to be offered in any good cause." She served as secretary of the Woman's Mission Circle, as the teacher of the Mistah Bible Class, and an active worker in the Bethany Circle. E.E. Masterman described Olive as "one of the noblest Christian characters I have ever known."[21]

Masterman also praised her charitable works. "She was always kind to everybody regardless of their station in life," he said. "She was deeply interested in charitable and philanthropic work, and she had a great practical sympathy for those in trouble. Her good works were never advertised or exploited, which made them shine all the brighter to those who knew of them." Indeed, she often cautioned friends, who chanced to know of her efforts, not to mention her charties. Yet many tons of coal were sent to poor families in wintertime, and many crippled or convalescing children were taken in her limousine for a drive through the city as a means of diverting their thoughts from their afflictions. Additionally, she demonstrated a special interest in the the very young

The picture of the Chandler children which Olive carried with her to the hospital in Chicago.

and the elderly who were hospitalized, often times making liberal, and anonymous, contributions to the hospital to enable them to receive proper medical treatment.[22]

When it was determined to have Olive submit to additional diagnosis and surgery, her first and last thoughts were of her children. Reportedly it was at their request that she agreed to undergo the second operation, and it was known that she took a group photograph of them along with her to the Chicago hospital. Following the surgery, a Wichita physician who also had accompanied her to Chicago, called on Mrs. Chandler before returning to Kansas. She "seemed very happy" and talked lovingly of her children. She even exacted a pledge from the doctor—that he would visit with the youngsters after reaching Wichita and assure them that mother Olive was progressing satisfactorily and soon would be home. She was a devoted mother to the end.[23]

The South Clifton residence was a lonely place for a father and four siblings (ages ranging from fourteen to nine) after Olive Thayer Chandler was buried on August 5, 1915, in Maple Grove Cemetery. To give direction to his home and to help manage the children, C.Q. had the good fortune to engage Mrs. Elizabeth McPherson, a fine woman of strong character and sensitivity. She was an excellent household manager and complemented C.Q.'s insistence on good manners and propriety at all times in personal demeanor. There was genuine respect between her and each of the five Chandlers.[24]

Before her death, Olive had contracted with Miss Floy Barnes to become the Chandler children's private tutor for the 1915 school year. The public schools were overcrowded, and Margaret still had difficulty getting around; thus, a home tutorial arrangement was thought to be essential because it was physically less demanding on her. Floy was a gifted teacher, but as time progressed, her influence proved more productive than just her educational assignment. One evening Mrs. McPherson became ill, and Miss Barnes was called to assume temporary management of the household. She brought with her Miss Alice Throckmorton, her roommate who taught at Lowell School, to assist with the children. It was the first meeting between C.Q. and Miss Alice, but neither envisioned what fate had in store for them.[25]

They were to meet several times over the next 18 months, but only informally in professional settings. Not until Miss Barnes resigned, effective at the end of the 1916-17 school year, was there reason for C.Q. to follow up on his acquaintance with Alice Throckmorton. He urged Miss Barnes to ask her roommate if she would be interested in considering the position. Meantime, C.Q. approached L.W. Mayberry, Superintendent of Wichita Schools, for a recommendation on Miss Throckmorton. Mayberry expressed high praise for her abilities and felt Chandler would be fortunate to employ her. An interview was arranged, and C.Q. was most impressed with her.[26]

The Throckmortons, he learned, were midwestern pioneers, having migrated to the territory before it became "bleeding Kansas." The family homesteaded near present Burlington in Coffey County, built a double log cabin, and became farmers in a difficult environment. George Throckmorton, Alice's father, attended the "school in Lawrence," but chose to become an agrarian like his father before him. He was typical of the small farmers of his day; he worked hard, provided adequately for his family, but had little or no cash flow even in years when harvests were good. Consequently, Alice was obliged to put herself through college, after which she found employment and financed her sister Nellie's education. Family legend holds that her sacrifice during those years was so extensive that she would allow herself but five cents per week as spending money.[27]

Eventually, Alice moved to Wichita and became a sixth grade teacher in the public schools. Social promotions were not characteristic of education in the early years of the 20th century, and she found several 14, 15, and 16 year-old students in her class, all with records of repeated failure, boredom, and bad conduct. She handled them with such skill that their demeanor and interest improved dramatically, and others with behavior problems from all over the school district soon were being sent to her classroom. To keep the boys occupied, Alice organized a basketball team, and to their surprise, she was able to outplay them at the sport. She was strong of mind and of body, and it was difficult for any student, regardless of age, not to show her respect or admiration.[28]

Alice was proud of her students, and she conveyed to C.Q. during their interview a sincere reluctance to leave them. After considerable discussion, Chandler became genuinely impressed with her intelligence and strength of character, and he formally extended to her a professional opportunity which was considerably more attractive financially than her public school position. To his disappointment, Alice politely and respectfully declined the offer. C.Q. refused to consider her response as final, and called on Superintendent Mayberry to use some helpful, friendly persuasion. Mayberry wrote Miss Throckmorton, urging her to reconsider, but her decision remained unchanged for a time. In February of 1917, C.Q. journeyed to Emporia, where Alice was visiting her younger sister, to discuss the matter again with her, and she finally consented to become the children's tutor for the following year.[29]

Chandler had made plans for the coming summer to take the children on a vacation to the east coast, in part because he felt it would be beneficial to Margaret's health. Since the trip was to be made by automobile, he needed a governess to help with the children, and he asked Miss Throckmorton if she would like to accompany them. Privately, C.Q. hoped the trip would bring the tutor and her students closer together before fall lessons began. Alice responded that she would be honored to accept if he would include her younger sister, Nellie, as her traveling companion, an arrangement which C.Q. thought most satisfactory.[30]

From the beginning of the trip, it was obvious that the children were comfortable with Alice and found it easy to show affection toward her. It was equally obvious that she "was taken" by them because she responded warmly to their attention. Such a development was pleasing to C.Q., and as their long, overland journey progressed, he and Alice occasionally talked about her professional responsibilities for the coming year, discussions which in time broadened to include topics of personal interest. They discovered many mutualities, including a firm commitment to Christian principles, and they also slowly became aware of the fact that they were falling deeply in love with each other.

Neither had anticipated or planned it, but both were too honest to hide their feelings once the truth was realized. By the time they had reached Atlantic City, Alice recognized that C.Q. was trying to find an opportunity to propose marriage, but each time he started in his halting, hesitant manner, "one of the kids would pop up" and spoil the mood. Finally, C.Q. called her room and asked her meet him at beachside where at last they found time to discuss their feelings without interruption. Admitting his love for her, he nonetheless expressed concern about the difference in their ages (he was 53, she was 27) should she consent to become his wife. She countered his concern with a confession of her own genuine affection as well as a convincing expression of ambivalence toward the age factor.

Alice accepted his proposal "and came floating back to her room," only to discover that Margaret, who had a delicate stomach, was quite ill after having eaten some shellfish and "was upchucking all over the place." In her happiness, Alice hardly recalled

Alice Throckmorton Chandler at the time of her marriage to C.Q. Chandler II in 1917.

that she worked for over an hour "cleaning up the mess" and getting Margaret settled into bed comfortably. It was the first acid test for the bride-to-be who was inheriting a ready-made family, but she proved then, as she would many times in the future, that she lovingly could manage difficult situations with the children without bothering their father. C.Q. did not learn of the dilemma until morning.

By the time the party started for Kansas, the matter of the impending marriage had been thoroughly discussed with the children, all of whom responded with enthusiastic approval. On their return trip they motored to the rural home of her parents, the George Throckmortons of Coffey County, Kansas, where they were married on September 5, 1917, by the Reverend Guy L. Brown, pastor of the First Baptist Church in Wichita who had driven to the Throckmorton home at Chandler's request to perform the ceremony.[31]

Thus, when the family returned to 200 South Clifton, Alice was C.Q.'s wife, not his children's tutor. When he suggested that they begin the search for a private school arrangement, she recommended instead that the children be placed in the public schools. "There is not a thing wrong with the school system in Wichita," she stated. "I've been teaching in it for years, and there is no reason for these children to go to a private school. They need the involvement with other children." She was persuasive. C.Q. respected her opinion so highly that he followed her advice and enrolled them in the Wichita schools, breaking with the past practice of educating his children at home.[32]

From the beginning, Alice was more than a surrogate mother. The summer experiences they all had shared and the excitement of starting a new life together made the adjustment easy for all of them. The new Mrs. Chandler treated the children as though they were her own, and they responded warmly to her love and devotion to their needs. Moreover, Alice supported C.Q. in every aspect of his life. C.Q. would record fourteen years after their marriage, "I can say from the depths of my heart she has made a wonderful Mother for the children and a one hundred percent wife and companion—surely God was good to us in sending her to us."[33]

Alice supported her husband's efforts to aid the crippled children in Kansas by entertaining them frequently at 200 South Clifton.

They became inseparable partners, sharing a deep faith and commitment to their Christian responsibilities as parents by always insisting on family participation in church services. Both came to be regarded as "pillars" in the First Baptist Church in Wichita. No task was too menial or involvement too demanding for either of them, and in the vernacular of the day, "they were known throughout the brotherhood as a faithful Christian couple who literally opened and closed the church house doors at each scheduled worship service or specially-called meeting."[34]

In later years, the Chandlers played a prominent role in persuading the Northern Baptist Convention to hold its 1941 annual convention in Wichita, a week-long event which brought much recognition and almost 5000 delegates from 36 states throughtout the Baptists' northern jurisdiction to the city. C.Q. was an active participant and rejoiced when an old pastor friend, Dr. William A. Elliott from Ottawa, Kansas, was elected president of the half-million member organization. Minnesota Governor Harold E. Stassen was chosen as vice president.[35]

William Allen White, publisher of the Emporia Gazette and Chandler's close friend, humorously referred to this picture as "the heavenly twins" because of their white suits.

Christmastime in 1925 at 200 South Clifton pictures L to R: standing, Charles Jerome, Margaret; seated, Mrs. C.J., William, Elizabeth, Mrs. C.Q. II; foreground, C.Q. II, Olive, George.

Alice also became active alongside her husband in the crippled children's movement. On numerous occasions, she opened her home to countless disabled children, hosting them for annual picnic lunches and then joining her husband in treating them to such exciting activities as the Ringling Brothers and Barnum and Bailey Circus or a sight-seeing flight (courtesy of Braniff Airways) over Wichita. Through the years, C.Q. drew high praise from prominent civic leaders everywhere, including such Kansans as journalist William Allen White as well as every governor of the state during the two decades he led the movement. "The Crippled Children of Kansas," a noted Kansas City physician wrote him, "owe you much, Mr. Chandler, and I am sure your name is written indelibly in the history of the State of Kansas." And so it was, but he would have been the first to acknowledge that the solid support he always received from Alice made his efforts doubly rewarding.[36]

C.Q. II and Alice with daughter Olive, who was named at the request of her older sisters after their deceased mother.

Such was the relationship they developed after their marriage in 1917—a sharing of all activities and a genuine, mutual respect for each other's interests. Even the matter of additional children, about which C.Q. at first felt uneasy because of his age, was resolved with maturity and affection. Chandler understood his young wife's need for fulfillment as a woman and mother, but she again was called upon to reassure him of her willingness to face the possibility of having to raise all their children alone. In time, she bore him a daughter and two sons: Olive on January 25, 1919; George

Throckmorton on February 1, 1921; and Anderson Woods on January 21, 1926.[37]

In raising two sets of children, Alice demonstrated remarkable sensitivity. She pulled them together as one family and discouraged all thoughts or behavior to the contrary. She masterfully handled her first pregnacy, calling the four children [Margaret, Charles, William, and Elizabeth] together and asking their help in selecting a name for the baby. "If I have a girl," she told them, "I want you girls to choose a name. If it is a boy, then you boys may select one." When she bore a daughter, Margaret and Elizabeth asked if the baby could be named Olive, after their mother. Alice, a wise and understanding woman, expressed her delight and followed their wishes; it was another solid link in the family chain. According to that child, now Mrs. Olive Chandler Clift, the children thereafter "were brought up as one big family and were very, very close, never regarding each other as half brothers or sisters. We had an absolutely, unbelievably happy childhood."[38]

Fortunately, C.Q.'s concern about his age was unfounded. Although he was approaching 55 when Olive was born, he would remain in vigorous health for over two decades, ample time to watch all of his children, except Anderson who was born in 1926, reach majority. Together, he and Alice provided stability and direction for their children in the tradition of a long lineage of Chandler families. However, the Chandler heritage was taking on new trappings; because of C.Q.'s emergence as one of the most influential bankers in the mid-continent region, his children found it difficult to resist the attractions of his profession. The Wichita Chandlers increasingly became known as "a banking family."

4

A COMMUNITY OF BANKS
AND RELATED INTERESTS

When C.Q. Chandler assumed control of the Kansas National Bank in Wichita, he announced that the KNB "was now part of a family affair." He made reference to himself, J.W. Berryman, E.E. Masterman, and W.S. Woods, all stockholders in the bank and all related to each other. By 1902, their holdings, separate and collective, embraced 18 banks in a "community extending from Humbolt, Kansas, to Clayton, New Mexico."[1] It was a budding empire of financial institutions, none of them large by modern measurements but strong nonetheless because of their common bond and the wise leadership of a conservative yet aggressive C.Q. Chandler.

In time the "community" would broaden to include almost three score banks, and C.Q.'s own maturing children (his sons directly, his daughters through marriage) would become important additions to "the family affair." In retrospect, his children's association with the banking profession seems almost inevitable in view of relevant data.[2] There was ample opportunity for them to find a niche in banking; from Chandler's historical notes and from other accounts, there is impressive list of at least 57 banks in 53 cities in five southwestern states in which he personally had "been interested, both financially and responsible for the management":

KANSAS

Ashland	Coldwater	Elkhart	Hunnewell	Medicine	South
Arkansas	Colony	Gueda	Kingman	Lodge	Haven
City	Coats	Springs	Liberal	Ottawa	Sharon
Altoona	Cheney	Garnett	Lyons	Penalosa	Spivey
Beaver	Dodge City	Greensburg	Madison	Pratt	Tyrone
Bucklin	Englewood	Hazelton	Meade	Preston	Wellington
Croft	Elk City	Hugoton		Quinlan	Wichita

A family of bankers, all related, standing L to R: C.E. Woods, W.S. Berryman, Paul S. Woods. Seated: J.W Berryman, C.Q. Chandler, W.S. Fallis. Picture taken at the Kansas Bankers Association meeting in 1903.

OKLAHOMA	TEXAS	COLORADO	NEW MEXICO
Alva	Booker	Holly	Clayton
Balko	Channing		
Billings	Higgins		
Carmen	Lipscomb		
Cherokee	McLean		
Gage	Perryton		
Pond Creek	Spearman		

In each of four Kansas cities—Ashland, Coldwater, Garnett, and Wichita—the Chandler interests at one time controlled two banks, some of which were merged, others later sold. C.Q.'s object in each case was to provide appropriate financial services for the communities in which the banks existed, and to extend through resident bank presidents the type of personalized assistance which businessmen and farmers needed, given the requirements of their environment. In those cases where the resources of the local banks were incapable of handling larger loan requests, those opportunities were referred to the Kansas National Bank in Wichita, in an arrangement not unlike contemporary correspondent banking.[3]

Thus, Chandler's developing banking community resembled an old Conestoga wagon wheel: numerous spokes ranging outward from the hub at Wichita. From the beginning however, he insisted that "every institution should stand on its own bottom." To accomplish that objective, he carefully selected capable young men and gave them the responsibility of running their banks. He insisted that each of them establish permanent residence in his respective community and become active in civic affairs. C.Q. was "a master builder," and he spent some part of each year visiting and helping to develop those young bank executives by sharing his experiences and imparting his philosophies to them. It was something of a marvel in the early days to see him motor up in his 1902 Oldsmobile, not only for his associates but also for school children in towns like Ashland whose schools were dismissed to allow first-hand viewing of the machine.[4]

During his visits, he urged young bank executives to study the business environment carefully and to follow enlightened, if conservative, guidelines in extending loans. His extraordinary interest and patience resulted in successful banking careers for numerous individuals who were quick to acknowledge their indebtedness to Chandler. "These younger men count themselves extremely fortunate," Frank Carr (a cousin who included himself among them) once remarked, "that in the trying times that often occur in this business, they have had the guiding hand of Mr. Chandler at the helm, and have had the opportunity to learn the fundamental principles under the watchful eye of so experienced a banker and businessman. They have resolved to carry on the traditions thus established, holding firmly to the idea of a safe bank for the depositors' money—the ideal of a true banker."[5]

By policy, each of the banks "had its own connections, its own lines of credit, and made its own investments independently. There was no intermingling of securities." The wisdom of such practices engendered confidence among bank employees and patrons alike, and built a type of stability which carried the Chandler banks through every business recession, including the Panic of 1907 and the Great Depression in 1929, without knowing failure.[6] Over the years, Chandler dismantled his community of banks, either because of the growing restrictions in banking regulations or because it seemed prudent to tighten his investment portfolio. A few of the banks were sold to members of his immediate family after they had gained sufficient experience to launch careers of their own.

As important as he felt the smaller banks were, C.Q. turned his attention increasingly to the Kansas National Bank. A growing city, expanding demands from the business community for financial assistance, and the corresponding need for greater efficiency in operations and record keeping put enormous pressure on banks with limited resources. However much C.Q. would have liked for the industry to remain highly personalized, he could no longer expect his profession to maintain the uncomplicated atmosphere he had enjoyed in his beloved Medicine Lodge. Modern banking practices in the larger cities like Wichita evolved in response to the emerging needs of those who were dependent upon financial assistance in shaping their businesses to meet rising consumer expectations.

Most men of vision can project the course of a continuum, but only the great ones are capable of adapting to it in timely, positive ways that permit them to take maximum advantage of the opportunities which are present in periods of change. From 1883 when he first entered the banking profession, C.Q. had demonstrated repeatedly that he was a man of vision with not only the ability to identify unmet needs but also the courage to assume the risks inherent in new ventures. After he arranged in 1900 to purchase the Kansas National in Wichita, he took control of a bank not much larger than the Citizens State in Medicine Lodge. However, he knew the potential of KNB, and he set about immediately to invest in its future, first making extensive renovations in the quarters it leased in the Citizen's Building, which was owned by a New Hampshire syndicate, and then purchasing the building outright a few years later.[7]

Thus, Chandler began his banking career in Wichita as president of a financial institution which had a long history of weathering difficult economic conditions. Indeed, the Kansas National Bank

Kansas National Bank in Wichita about 1900, looking west.

hardly could be regarded as "the new kid on the block," for it had its beginnings in 1876 when Hiram W. Lewis founded the Farmer's and Merchant's Bank as a private corporation. Early successes occasioned reorganization in 1882, and Lewis secured a federal charter under a new name: the Kansas National Bank. However, business vacillations in a typical nineteenth-century cowtown like Wichita were characterized by periods of optimism and prosperity followed by despair and recession. Such were to be Lewis' experiences.

Lewis successfully met an economic downturn in 1883-84, and then led the bank to record earnings during a real estate and construction boom in 1887-88. He even overcame a loss in confidence among some bank officials over his private dealings in real estate because they were "so closely connected with the activities of the bank." He separated those interests from the KNB and profited greatly, but prosperity for both him and the bank was shortlived. Another recession in 1889 placed enormous pressure on the bank's ability to meet its obligations and to liquidate its loans, some of which were owed by Hiram Lewis, the bank's president. Thereafter, his continuation in that position became difficult.

He resigned in 1891, and the KNB struggled through hard times until James O. Davidson, who controlled the Citizen's Bank in Wichita, bought stock in the Kansas National. Davidson effected a merger of the two institutions in 1895 under the Kansas National name and moved all operations to the Citizen's Building at Main and Douglas. Even then, the bank struggled, and its major stockholders sought repeatedly either to sell the bank or to merge it with other Wichita banks until C.Q. Chandler and his "banking family" purchased it in 1900.

A period of enlightened leadership and judicious promotion followed. Deposits grew, and loans expanded. By 1905 the KNB regularly paid a 3% quarterly dividend, but care was taken "to make sure that gains for the bank were solid and conservative." C.Q. became active in the Wichita Clearing House Association, an organization begun in 1888 to facilitate the handling and exchanging of checks drawn on the various banks in the city, and he became a strong advocate of interbank cooperation in an era of growing complexity in banking operations. Again, there were good times and bad, the latter highlighted in early developments by a numbing panic in 1907 during which specie became so scarce that the Kansas National Bank was obliged to issue cashier's checks for such sums as 25 cents as change in small transactions.[8] Happily, there were better times ahead.

By 1910, L.S. Naftzger, a respected Wichita banker in his own right, would write that the KNB "has safely come through the financial storm" and that it "still is one of the most solid, substantial, and conservative financial institutions in the state ... and has its own building at the corner of Main Street and Douglas Avenue." The bank, Naftzger recorded, "is under the able and efficient management of C.Q. Chandler, president; E.E. Masterman, vice president; J.W. Berryman, second vice president; Elsberry Martin, cashier; and Charles Testard, assistant cashier."[9] Chandler had successfully met and recovered from the most severe challenge of his banking career.

Thus, a decade after he purchased the bank, C.Q.'s reputation as a sound manager was fully established, but he admitted that he "was still learning." Over the 27 years he had been involved in the business, he had observed that banks with limited resources often

Wichita Clearing House Association in 1907, seated L to R: A.C. Jobes (President, National Bank of Commerce), L.S. Naftzger (President, Fourth National Bank), J.N. Richardson (President, Clearing House Association). Standing: C.Q. Chandler (President, Kansas National Bank), V.H. Branch (Cashier, Fourth National Bank).

suffered more losses during periods of "bust" than they could reasonably recover in times of "boom." He had witnessed many failures, and had watched the strong absorb the weak in a type of consolidation born of adversity—or of necessity—or of both. To a man of vision, the pattern was as indelible as the solution was obvious: grow, or remain a high risk factor in a difficult industry.

Growth for growth's sake, however, was anathema to C.Q. He believed that only such expansion as was reasoned and orderly would contribute to the actual stability of any financial institution. Size alone was no buffer against failure. For those who disagreed, he had only to point to the demise in 1876 of the First National Bank of Wichita which boasted of its $2,000,000 in deposits (by far the largest in Wichita at the time) but which nonetheless failed after it overextended itself in cattle paper, and after it financed a costly, but poorly located, new bank building to which the community would not come in sufficient numbers to do business.[10]

Chandler was a strong advocate of an unregulated market place,

Frank Overton Carr, cousin of C.Q. Chandler II, was Vice President and Cashier of First National at the time of his retirement in 1955.

and as harsh as it seemed to some, he even accepted the principle that weak or poorly-managed businesses should be allowed to fail if they were unable to meet the conditions of open competition. He also believed that such failures actually strengthened the free enterprise system. Nowhere is this philosophy more in evidence than in the spirited way he led the lobby efforts of the Kansas Bankers Association in fighting against legislative attempts to regulate the industry. Despite his ardor and that of other KBA members, regulations came increasingly from both Topeka and Washington, but Chandler again was counted as being among those with sufficient vision to analyze the trends and project what might happen

Frank Lee Carson who ultimately rose to become President and Chairman of the Board of First National.

in the future. It was obvious to him that banking had entered an age characterized not only by consolidation and interbank cooperation but also by increasing politicization. Being active in politics, at least to the extent of attempting to shape the laws which governed the industry, became an accepted obligation for most bank presidents as well as many directors and stockholders.

Chandler spent his share of time in the tribunals, but he was careful to keep all such commitments in perspective. His first priority was the health of the KNB, and he, along with E.E. Masterman and J.W. Berryman, became the nucleus around which the bank was organized and operated. Together they built wisely, not just in bank assets but in professional personnel as well. They were ably supported by two important men who were retained in their positions when the bank was purchased: Elsberry Martin (cashier) and Charles Testard (assistant cashier). There were others, some of whom were younger men.[11]

Frank Overton Carr, another of Chandler's cousins who also was a native of C.Q.'s hometown of Rocheport, Missouri, moved in 1901 with his family to Wellington, Kansas, where a year later he graduated from Sumner County High School. He worked for the Kansas National during the summers of 1903 and 1904, then joined the bank on a full time basis in 1905. He was given assignments "all over the bank" until he was promoted in 1915 to assistant cashier. He earned and commanded everyone's highest respect, including that of C.Q. Chandler who made him a director on January 31, 1918, and thereafter gave him increasing responsibilities as the bank expanded to become the region's leading financial institution.[12]

Frank Lee Carson also was an important addition to the team of men whom Chandler recruited to help build the KNB. His parents were not native to the state, having moved from Illinois to Kansas in 1885. Frank finished Ashland High School in 1909 and attended Washburn College and the University of Kansas from which he received his A.B. Degree in 1913. Carson wanted to be a banker, and on the advice of J.W. Berryman, he moved to Wichita and studied shorthand and typewriting at the Wichita Business College. Chandler was impressed with him and employed him for a short time to do clerical work for the First Baptist Church, after which Frank accepted a temporary assignment with the Coldwater National Bank. Finally on Labor Day in 1914, Chandler invited him to join the staff of Kansas National, and a long and rewarding association with the master banker began. Carson eventually would become president of the bank, and upon C.Q.'s death in 1943 would succeed Chandler as chairman of the board.[13]

Frank Carr and Frank Carson were ambitious, if inexperienced, young men who had committed themselves to banking careers. C.Q. was impressed with their dedication. They willingly began at the bottom, eagerly accepted any assignment given them, and quickly took advantage of every opportunity to improve their skills. And they profited most from those times when they were fortunate enough to work directly with Chandler. A venerable and wise bank president, knowing the importance of providing continuity to the direction of the bank, gave them much attention and carefully prepared them to become future leaders. They acknowledged his "gift" with hard work and genuine respect; he responded to their loyalty with admiration and increasing responsibility.[14]

While he was expanding a staff which he knew would constitute a second generation of leadership, Chandler took a major step in developing the KNB. Convinced that size was important to future stability in the highly competitive Wichita marketplace, C.Q. entered into negotiations with officials of the National Bank of Commerce, located across the street on the southwest corner of Douglas and Main. NBC was ably managed by Charles W. Carey and was successful enough to pay its officers high salaries and its stockholders attractive semi-annual dividends. The directors of the two banks obviously believed that a merger would benefit both institutions, for a consolidation was effected in 1919 under the designation of the Kansas National Bank of Commerce, making the new entity, with its $1 million in both capital stock and surplus and its $16 million in combined deposits, equal to if not greater in size than any of Wichita's existing banks. It was a step of major significance.[15]

By the terms of the merger, KNB shareholders received 60% of the new stock issue, and C.Q. Chandler was made Chairman of the Board and Executive Manager. Thereafter, the new bank's organizational chart reflected the prudent utilization of the combined staffs' proven managerial talents. Four vice presidencies were created to administer specialized divisions, and F.L. Carson, the relative newcomer, was given the important post of cashier. Not surprisingly, Frank Carr was assigned to one of seven assistant cashierships, positions which themselves represented the growing complexities of operating a large financial institution.

Shortly after the consolidation, discussions were held with federal banking authorities on the subject of a name change for the bank, and Chandler specifically inquired about the possibility of renaming it the First National Bank since Wichita at the time had no bank with that designation. There were some complications. Federal policy precluded the reissuance of a name previously used in a city, and the initial First National Bank of Wichita had vacated that title after its failure in 1876. Chandler persisted and convinced the Comptroller of the Currency that Wichita's oldest surviving bank deserved the name First National, provided the technicalities in the policy could be met. A semantic compromise resulted—The First National Bank in (not "of") Wichita—and the name was approved and issued as a replacement for The Kansas National Bank of Commerce.[16]

The consolidation and name change presaged a new era for the Wichita bank. Indeed, the decade following the merger was one of growth and change, not only for First National but also for Wichita and the nation as well. It was, as Frank Carr reflected in 1935, the "Golden Age" which "witnessed the greatest expansion of business that has ever been known." The First grew as Wichita grew, its welfare being "indissolubly bound up with that of its community." Chandler's KNB, before the merger, listed almost $20 million in total assets; by 1929 the First National would boast of over $30 million, a growth that did not go unnoticed outside of Wichita and Kansas. By the end of the period, Chandler was being referred to as a "nationally known financial genius."[17]

Fiscal growth was accompanied by physical expansion. Almost before the ink had dried on the consolidation agreement, Chandler and his associates were studying future space needs. They were sensitive also about the public image they wished to project for their growing giant. Major eastern bank buildings were substantial structures and purposely appointed to reflect stability and promote confidence among depositors and the business community. C.Q. envisioned a new structure of similar image but, hopefully, less extravagant. He invited C.E. Richards, a partner in a Columbus, Ohio, architectural firm, to present to the bank's directors a design for a structure which would afford them "very suitable rooms with some rental space" within a cost range significantly lower than what eastern bankers normally allocated for their buildings. The directors were pleased with what the architect proposed.

Richards was engaged, the plans were drawn, and Chandler negotiated firm leases for needed lots adjacent to the KNB properties on the northwest corner of Douglas and Main where the new structure would be located. To make way for the construction, all bank-

*Temporary home
(1919) of the First
National Bank, located
directly south of the
present FNB building.*

The First National Bank, looking east, during the period of construction.

ing operations were moved across the street to the National Bank of Commerce building "for the duration." The project proved anything but easy. Frustrating construction delays, extensive cost overruns, and occasional indecisiveness by both bankers and builders plagued the project. Richards urged Chandler not to allow his impatience with construction schedules to cause him to sacrifice quality, reasoning "that the building would be a Wichita fixture for a long time to come, and during all that time it would influence the image of the bank."[18]

Unfortunately, Richards died before the project was completed, but his philosophies prevailed. Construction proceeded much slower than anticipated, and in the end, the directors spent more than they intended—but they got a finer building than they had expected. The final $1.4 million price tag on the ten-story ediface was almost twice the costs the directors originally had projected, but the new home of the First National Bank in Wichita was a showplace of design and decoration. As Craig Miner has written, "When the new building opened on March 16, 1922, the 40,000 visitors to the new facility already imagined what the years have confirmed,

The First National Bank in Wichita, as completed in 1922.

that the decision not to compromise quality was ultimately a wise one." Again, Chandler had built for permanency.[19]

A maturing C.Q. Chandler's professional stature increased as the decade lengthened. Once during a minor economic crisis in 1924 when a sister bank was threatened with runs on its deposits, he went personally to the lobby of that institution, mounted a chair amid frenzied depositors, and announced that the bank was sound, that their funds were not in jeopardy, and that they should return home. His reputation as a financial expert, coupled with the fact that he was then president of the Clearing House Association, turned the "run"into a walk—toward the door instead of the money cages. Reassured and satisfied depositors calmly left the bank.[20]

His visibility as a business and community leader inevitably marked him as a logical candidate for public office. As early as 1921, Kansas Governor Henry J. Allen privately inquired about his availability as a candidate for the state's top post. In time, other influential Republicans urged him to consider the race, but after giving it his "most careful, prayerful consideration," C.Q. declined the opportunity. "If I thought it was service instead of honor," he wrote Allen, "it might be different. I do not feel the call to service in this matter." Perhaps his wife, Alice, offered a better explanation when she advised her banker husband, "You would make a good governor, but you would be very unhappy in such a position."[21]

At least three opportunities for federal service also were extended to him during the twenties. In 1926-27, he was invited by Colonel J.W. McIntosh, Comptroller of the Currency, to consider an appointment to the Federal Reserve Board, a discussion which was shrouded in confidentiality over an extended period. Ultimately, C.Q. withdrew from consideration because the appointment required divestment of all his bank stock and precluded participation in the banking business for two years after retiring from the board. McIntosh tried again in 1927, urging Chandler to consider a board appointment to the important Farm Loan Board, but that offer also was respectfully declined. Finally, in 1928 the Wichita banker was mentioned prominently as the "the logical choice" for appointment to the unexpired term of Kansas Senator Charles Curtis, Herbert Hoover's running mate in the November presidential elections. An old dispute surfaced between the Senator and governor-elect Clyde Reed and delayed Curtis' early resignation; C.Q. saw it as his opportunity to withdraw quietly from further consideration. He knew that such an interim appointment most often is a cameo assignment, an honor extended to a prominent party faithful who dutifully declines to become a candidate for the

Banquet held in lobby of the new FNB building shortly after its completion in 1922.

C.Q. II took an active interest in national politics. Here he is shown with Warren G. Harding in August of 1920, along with his son Billy Chandler.

post when general elections are held. It was the type of honor Chandler did not covet, nor did he have the time to devote even to a brief assignment in Washington.[22]

C.Q. was a busy man indeed for a person past sixty. He not only had his banking activities, which expanded during the 1920s to include numerous banks in Kansas, Oklahoma, Texas, and Colorado, but also had two other major business interests which required attention. In March of 1905, before he moved his family from Medicine Lodge, Chandler invested with other Wichita businessmen in a grain merchandising operation, which was named the Red Star Milling Company. The new venture was a marginal enterprise for the first three years, but enjoyed a spectacular growth in revenues and surplusses after L.R. Hurd, an experienced and knowledgeable miller, was persuaded in 1908 to become the operations manager. By 1919, C.Q. owned 42% of a company which was approaching a half-million dollars in annual net profits, and whose principal product, Red Star Flour, was enjoying unparalleled popularity among area patrons.[23]

Major investors also took note of the success of the product. By 1926, Goldman, Sachs and Company of New York City made an offer to purchase Red Star, but Chandler and Hurd were unimpressed with the price Goldman placed on the stock. A short time later, the Pillsbury Milling Company of Minneapolis expressed an interest in acquiring the Mill, but that contact also proved fruitless. Then in May of 1928, a new contact came from James F. Bell, a representative of the Washburn-Crosby Company, which milled "Gold Medal" flour in plants located in Minneapolis, Buffalo, Kansas City, Chicago, and Louisville. At a meeting on May 8 in St. Paul between officers of the two companies, Bell submitted a proposition calling for a consolidation of Red Star, Washburn-Crosby, and a Wichita Falls, Texas, firm owned by Frank Kell. A tentative agreement for a new company to be known as General Mills was reached, but Kell later declined to approve it, nullifying the deal.[24]

Bell was persistent. A second conference was arranged for June 14 at the Lucern Hotel in Kansas City, Missouri, this time without Kell but with representatives of other western milling companies, and a second proposal was drafted which offered $273.50 per share to holders of Red Star common stock. Two meetings later, both of which were held at the Ritz-Carlton Hotel in New York City, the agreement was ratified. Red Star thereafter became a part of General Mills, Inc., a new $50 million corporation which also merged Wasburn-Crosby, the Royal Milling Company, the Rocky Mountain Elevator Company of Montana, and the Kalispell Flour Mills Company, also of Montana.[25]

Final negotiations resulted in a tender of $275 per share for Red Star stock, of which Chandler held 5000 shares, giving him a net capital gain before taxes of almost $1.2 million. According to a carefully detailed ledger, C.Q. made an interesting and unselfish disposition of his earnings. He allotted almost $200,000 to various charitable causes, chief among which was the Chandler Benevolent Society for Crippled Children. Over a half million dollars, in designated shares, were place in trust for Alice and their seven children, and gifts totalling $28,700 were given to seven associates and employees, including F.L. Carson, F.O. Carr, A.L. Wood, Charles Testard, and Leland Scrogin, each of whom received $5000. A final ledger entry, approximately $300,000, was listed only as "investments."[26]

Thus the year 1928 witnessed the termination of C.Q.'s involvement in one business endeavor, and an acceleration of his activities in another—the Northwestern Mutual Life Insurance Company of Milwaukee, Wisconsin. Chandler's first involvement with Northwestern Mutual began in 1895 as a holder of policy #335332. In subsequent years, he purchased additional life insurance from NMLIC, not knowing that his policies one day would qualify him for membership on a unique committee. The company's by-laws provided for a five-member Board of Examiners, appointed from "policy holders who have no other interest in the company" and selected "with an eye to geographical and professional variance." C.Q. was tapped in 1927 for service on that Board which had the responsibility of conducting annual internal audits of company policies and conduct.[27]

William D. Van Dyke, president of the company, obviously was impressed with C.Q.'s work on the committee. When a vacancy occurred on NMLIC's Board of Trustees in 1928, Van Dyke nominated Chandler for the position, and he was duly elected on July 16, 1928, to fill an unexpired, three-year term. It was the beginning of a long professional service to the company which would not end until August 5, 1942, when an aging C.Q. finally retired from the Board.[28]

Perhaps the greatest of his contributions during that period occurred in 1932. Until then, Northwestern Mutual had enjoyed steady growth under the leadership of William Van Dyke, but his death on June 7, 1932, left the company without a president and with an executive committee sharply divided on who should be named to replace him as head of the billion dollar firm. Rumors circulated that President Calvin Coolidge was being considered, but insiders knew that there were at least three factions within the Board, each favoring a separate candidate. The selection still was unsettled in September when Chandler took the initiative to write each Board member, urging them to consider meeting a day in advance of the October Trustees' meeting in an effort to break the deadlock.[29]

The response was unanimous, and at a special session on October 18, 1932, chaired by Chandler, the Wichita banker skillfully led the 24 members present through individual and open discussions before he gave them his personal evaluation of the various candidates. He concluded with a convincing statement of support for Michael J. Cleary, NMLIS vice president since 1919, so strong in fact that during the official Board meeting the next morning, all of the trustees voted in favor of Cleary. It was a wise selection, and even though Cleary remarked that "1932 was a dickens of a time to be elected president of anything," he ably led the company through the depression, posting significant gains each year. And, Chandler was rewarded with a seat on the all-important Executive Committee for his positive leadership.[30]

If 1932 was a difficult time for insurance executives, it was no less so for bank presidents. As the nation's economy worsened in the early months of 1933, many financial institutions in Kansas faced heavy withdrawals by their depositors and were struggling to survive. As a measure of relief, Governor Alfred Landon imposed emergency restrictions on state banks, limiting depositors to withdrawals of no more than 5% of their funds. National banks were not necessarily affected by the proclamation, but Chandler reluctantly complied with the order, even though the First National was in a sound cash position and would remain so during the national bank holiday declared by President Franklin Roosevelt in March of 1933.[31]

The decade which followed was a period of deflation marked by a liquidation of loans and a decline in the demand for money. The First National suffered a reduction in income and was obliged to reduce rates on savings accounts, but its stability was never threatened. "Security results from consistent philosophies and prudent investment policies," Chandler always maintained, "and conservative banking is the only kind of banking we know." But to complete the analysis, he would also include the importance of surrounding himself with competent associates.[32]

His strongest supporter throughout the troubled thirties was his bank's president, Frank Lee Carson, who had succeeded C.W. Carey

*The depression did not prevent Will Rogers from accepting C.Q.'s invitation
to speak at a convention for crippled children in Wichita in April of 1933.*

following his death in 1927. "Carey was a most excellent man," C.Q.
wrote upon his passing, "and one of the best judges of security I
have ever come in contact with." His loss to the bank was great, but
it would have been even more severe had he not joined with Chandler in recognizing and developing Carson's talents. They did their
work well; Carson became an outstanding leader alongside his aging mentor.[33]

Chandler and Carson were precisely the combination the First
National needed in difficult times. Both were outgoing, gregarious
individuals whose poise exuded confidence and whose sincere demeanor added a personal touch in their dealings with customers.
They were always accessible. "Mr. Chandler," Zula B. Greene wrote
in 1935, "is a kindly, smiling, happy man who sits at his wide ma-
hogany desk and talks to people with as leisurely an interest as the

village loafer." Olive Chandler, his youthful daughter, may have misinterpreted her father's style but described it well when she said, "I can't see that Papa works any. All he does is swing around in his chair and talk to people."

Carson also was people oriented. He was known by everyone for his "exceptionally pleasing personality," and for a slight but noticeable limp when he walked. Although he had a private office, he frequently would position himself at a desk near the Main Street entrance and hail every customer who entered the door. His "hello John, how are you" type of greeting could be heard clearly throughout the lobby, and the gesture left patrons with a feeling of warmth and personal worth by causing them to reflect privately, "Why, that's Mr. Carson; he's president of the bank; he knows me." Even in difficult business decisions, his personality was such that could he turn down an individual's loan request and have the person "walk out of his office singing his praise." Frank made many friends for the bank and clearly became identified as the leader of a second generation of First National officials.[35]

That second generation was expanding, and along with Carson and Frank Carr, names such as Paul Woods and Charles Jerome Chandler, C.Q.'s oldest son, were added to the list of younger employees who would form the nucleus of a third. The combined talents of these men were the type of assets whose value cannot be shown on financial statements, but they were evident in other important ways. For example, the *Wichita Evening Eagle* summarized the status of the First National in 1937 by emphasizing the role of its leadership over the decade since 1927:

> This year there ends a decade as trying to all phases of American life as any in peacetime history. Brave institutions without number have disappeared forever since that ominous crack of doom in 1929. But many others have weathered the lean years to emerge now, firmer, stronger, greater than ever, their sinews tempered by the battering elements of economic disaster.
>
> One of Wichita's outstanding examples of triumphant survival and progress in the face of adversity is The First National Bank in Wichita, established in, and an integral part of this city since 1876—61 years!
>
> Officers of that bank will tell you that 1927 ... [was] the peak of

Earl Evans (right) and C.Q., longtime friends, shared a visit with President Herbert Hoover in Wichita.

their accomplishments. Yet, in 1937, ... after seven merciless years that ravaged men and their money, they will show you that the bank's deposits are over $10,100,000 greater than they were then; that the total assets are higher by over $10,200,000 than in 1927.

They will add, too, that even now the banking picture is not what it should be, specific testimony that this accomplishment has not been the product of chance or the mysterious workings of a benevolent fate ... that it has been due to the keen judgment, the sound policies and the unfaltering guidance through stormy waters by C.Q. Chandler, chairman of the board now, and his fellow officers of the bank.[36]

Little wonder that sobriquets such as "the nationally known financial genius" were often used in news accounts of Chandler's banking achievements, or that he was one of only two Wichitans (the other was his longtime friend Earl W. Evans) whose biographies were included in the 1936 edition of *Eminent Americans,* an exclusive "blue book" listing 800 nationally-prominent business and professional personalities. His work at First National was significant enough, the publication emphasized, but it was difficult to ignore the fact that he had been president of over 50 banks in the southwest, 27 of them at one time, during his illustrious career. He was recognized further in 1938 by being elected unanimously to membership on the Federal Advisory Council for the Tenth Federal Reserve District, the first such designation for an individual "outside Kansas City." The *Wichita Beacon* hailed the appointment

The banking cousins'Old World tour in 1929, showing L to R: native guides, J.W. Berryman, C.Q. Chandler, W.S. Fallis, and W.S. Berryman, on the steps of the Egyptian Museum in Cairo.

as "recognition of his outstanding record as a banker," and as "an honor in which Wichita and Kansas proudly share."[37]

Despite the accolades, C.Q. obviously felt by 1937 that the time had come to allow the younger men to assume the major responsibilities in the bank, for he began to spend more and more time in pursuing interests of a personal nature, especially in enjoying one of his favorite pasttimes—traveling. C.Q. had done his share of foreign tours during the twenties, having taken Alice in 1924 on a delayed honeymoon/sightseeing trip to Europe. Later in 1929, he and four of his cousins, J.W. Berryman, W.S. Fallis, W.S. Berryman, and W.M. Price, made a 60-day old world tour on which "neither politics nor business" was allowed to interfere with a relaxed trip through the Mediterranean, with calls on "the Holy Land, Gibralter, Athens, Cairo, Naples, Venice, and Rome," as well as "an

William A. (Billy) Sunday, a prominent evangelist of his day, was a guest in the Chandler home in 1930.

airplane trip from Cairo to Baghdad." And, he made a third trip to Europe in 1936 with his 15-year-old son, George, which was a highlight in the early life of the young high school junior. C.Q. could have enjoyed many more such experiences, but he preferred seeing the wonders of his own country, especially those in the southwest.[38]

Although he frequently rode the train when attending professional meetings and occasionally flew when time and work schedules made it expedient, he almost was addicted to the use of an automobile because of the conveniences it afforded him as a tourist. C.Q. was an avid sightseer, and he rarely made a business trip without arranging a side trip for personal enjoyment.

When he increased the frequency of his automobile excursions after 1937, he found an enthusiastic partner in Victor Murdock, publisher of the *Wichita Eagle*. They had begun their motor trips together in 1926 by staging annual business/pleasure visits into the wheatlands around Wichita and, over time, extending them to include a much wider region, including such interesting geographical phenomena as the Flint Hills and the gypsum mines near Sun City. Chandler usually took time to call on the banks of the areas visited, and Murdock wrote descriptive accounts of their experiences which often were published in his newspapers—but their trips were made mostly for pleasure. Both were history buffs, and they loved to visit historic sites and make inquiries into the legends of early Kansas. Several trips were made during the years of the dust bowl, and some memorable photographs of the devastated farms and towns survive in Chandler's memorabilia.[39]

One excursion Chandler made in 1938 was a poignant attempt to pay homage to his "roots." He and Alice drove "on a trip of nostalgia" to Green Springs Valley in Louisa County, Virginia, the site from which his grandparents, Leroy and Sarah Ann Quarles Chandler, and their large family had embarked in 1836 in covered wagons for permanent settlement in Missouri. The diary Sarah kept on that trek had been in C.Q.'s possession for many years, and he and his family occasionally read and marvelled at the hardships their pioneering ancestors had endured. When portions of the 100-year-old diary were serialized in 1935 in the *Boonville (Missouri) Advertiser*, C.Q.'s sense of adventure was aroused.

Nothing would sate his love of history and heritage except to retrace that journey in the comfort of his modern Buick. Thus in November of 1938, after visiting the old homesite in Virginia for a few days, the Chandlers used a highway map as a guide and motored along a route which closely approximated the entries in Sarah's diary. Each evening, in the form of letters which he addressed "Dear Grandmother," C.Q. wrote brief accounts of their experiences, all of which fortunately have been perserved. He recorded that they found little difficulty in identifying many of the sights she had described, but that they were humbled when they compared their conditions with those described in the diary. For example, on November 30 he wrote:

> You had each night, "the commotion of fixing the tents, cooking, etc.," and the "confusion of tongues not inferior to the clack of Babel" when you needed rest. We stopped our smooth running Buick car in front of a mammoth hotel. Two minutes later we were

comfortably settled in a steam-heated room with a tiled wash room and bath.... You slept frequently on wet bedding and tried to keep your twelve children well and at peace. What a task it must have been with Louisa only four months old, and Sarah Ann, John, James, Mary, Margaret, Eloisa, Timothy and Charles all less than eleven years of age. I wish you could have enjoyed these fresh beds with inner spring mattresses and light woolen blankets.

For C.Q., the trip was an experience in humility. "Your courage," he concluded, "fills me with awe. We'll try to live worthy of such a heritage."[40]

Beginning in 1939, the number of his automobile trips increased dramatically, and his itineraries sometimes carried him and others thousands of miles on journeys extending over several days. Chandler always made the arrangements and furnished the car, and Murdock shared as many of the trips as his schedule would permit. In November of 1939, their annual trip was extended to include parts of Oklahoma and New Mexico. In May of 1940, they crossed Oklahoma and drove southward into Texas, going as far as Menard where they visited the old San Saba Mission. Chandler sandwiched in a three-week excursion in August with a member of his board to view Mount Rushmore in South Dakota and see the Grand Coulee Dam in Washington. Still later in November of that year, he, Murdock, A.L. Wood and son Will Chandler made a week-long trip into the Mississippi Delta, visiting Natchez and New Orleans and other scenic locales.[41]

In June of the following year, Chandler invited his son-in-law, Robert Clogston, to accompany him, Murdock, and Wood in motoring through Missouri where they made stops, among other places, at Rocheport and New Madrid, the site of a 19th century earthquake which altered the flow of the Mississippi River until an enormous crevice (now known as Reelfoot Lake) was filled. November found them again in New Mexico on a trip which was highlighted by a visit to the Carlsbad Caverns. In October, C.Q. and Alice travelled to Louisville, Kentucky, to attend a crippled childrens' convention, but in November, Chandler, Murdock, and Wood were again in Texas, reaching Galveston on the Gulf coast, Presidio on the Mexican border, and historic El Paso on the Rio Grande before returning to Wichita.[42]

Victor Murdock, publisher of the Wichita Eagle, was a frequent traveling companion. He and C.Q. are pictured at Bagnall Dam in 1941.

As enjoyable as the trips were, they nonetheless were strenuous for a 77-year-old man. No venture of major significance was recorded during 1942, and unfortunately, failing health in 1943 precluded any serious thoughts of one during that year. C.Q.'s health declined noticeably in the last months of 1943, then suddenly grew much worse in December. He was admitted to Wesley Hospital, and on December 17, doctors listed his condition as critical. His family gathered about him as his strength waned, but their encouragement could not reverse the inevitable. The end came quietly on Sunday, December 19, shortly before midnight.[43]

A community mourned, and respect was shown in numerous ways for a departed comrade. The Rotary Club of Wichita, in which Chandler was a longtime participant, stood at its Monday noon meeting in silent tribute to his memory. The Clearing House Association announced that all Wichita banks would close on Tuesday afternoon as a memorial to his distinguished career. Condolences, written and verbal, flooded the Chandler home and scores of business and professional men came from other cities to attend the funeral services on December 21 at the First Baptist Church.[44]

The ceremony was sensitively officiated by Reverend Lewis M. Hale, who read C.Q.'s favorite biblical passages and summarized his personal feelings by saying, "In the archives of my own memory, no words I have heard from Mr. Chandler's lips will linger longer or speak more eloquently than these: 'God has been good to me'." C.Q. was laid to rest, in a private ceremony, at the family plot in Maple Grove Cemetery.[45]

For 38 years, it was said in numerous newpaper articles, Chandler was outstanding in the life of Wichita, almost four decades of service and rare achievement in which "his civic endeavors, finance, philanthropy and depth of devotion to his fellow citizens" were exemplary and beyond estimate. He had been a busy man, the *Topeka State Journal* editorialized, and some of his countless civic activities and philanthropies were not well known. "But," it concluded, "he always had time for things of that sort. Busy men are that way."[46]

Chandler's death closed the first chapter in the history of the First National Bank, and even though he had been the principal scribe, he knew that he had not written his portion of the book alone. Younger penmen, whom he carefully selected and trained, had helped him immeasurably and now awaited the opportunity to add their own chapters of achievement to the story.

5

C.Q. and C.J.: THE LEGEND AND HIS SUCCESSOR

C.Q. Chandler's life had been one of consistent endorsement of the philosophy that "all past is prologue," a belief that yesterday's achievements provide a platform for launching tomorrow's objectives. The respect he held for his ancestry was an unmistakable hallmark in his personality: he was proud to have been born a Chandler. He wore the name with honor and accepted unhesitatingly the obligations imposed on a patriarch who bears for his generation the responsibility of preserving an appreciation for ancestral ties and traditions. Still, he had reason to be proud of his own successes, because they had added by far the greatest prestige and affluence ever realized by a family whose accumulated achievements dated to the earliest settlements in colonial Virginia. A lesser man would have gloried in that feat, but the test of C.Q.'s convictions can be measured by the preparations he made for that December day when his accomplishments became a part of the prologue.

The value of his estate was not made public upon his death in 1943, but Chandler was reported at the time to have been one of the wealthiest men in Kansas. Affluence, however, had never threatened the foundations of his character, for he believed that life was a gift from God which should be lived in harmony with His teachings. No one knew scriptural admonitions about the dangers of wealth better than C.Q., and throughout his life, he taught his children by example that the boots of good fortune must be laced with strong strands of humility and responsible stewardship. Only then, he wrote late in life, would any of them prove worthy of the sacrifices their ancestors had made in inhospitable environments while paving the road along which subsequent generations could walk toward new challenges and enriching opportunities. Certainly C.Q. was grateful to his fore-bears, and he was confident that his children were amply pre-pared to carry on the family's traditions. That faith was stated in substantive, if simple, terms in his will.[1]

Chandler's Last Will and Testament was an uncomplicated expression of love and trust. After all reasonable debts and taxes were paid, 95 percent of the residuary value of his estate, in-cluding bank holdings but exclusive of life insurance, was be-queathed in equal shares to Mrs. Chandler and their seven children, to be held in trust by the First National Bank and ad-ministered by his wife and two oldest sons, Charles Jerome and William W. Chandler. According to the wordage in the docu-ment, Alice insisted that she not be allotted a portion greater than the others, although she was given possession of the family residence and furnishings at 200 South Clifton. The remaining five percent of the estate was awarded to the Chandler Benev-olent Society whose trustees were given full discretionary powers to distribute the funds among the various charities normally supported by the society, including the crippled children's movement.[2]

The legacy C.Q. left his progeny was more than his accumu-lated wealth and the control of the various banks he owned. They also were inheritors of proven banking practices and philoso-phies which had been shared with them for over four decades, and of an enriched Chandler heritage which he had taken con-siderable pains to document. However, no research was neces-sary to confirm that the Chandler surname had become the identifying cognomen for the clan in the 20th century because of the impact of C.Q.'s phenomenal successes, but the patriarch himself was aware that he had not been alone in writing the fam-ily name into the annals of the financial world. There were many talented relatives, with surnames other than Chandler and with forebears equally as industrious, who had played prominent roles in developing the "community of banks out in Kansas."

Indeed, a resourceful family member—his uncle W.S. Woods—in 1883 had encouraged C.Q. to move to Kansas, and Woods would remain associated with his nephew in many of the early acquisitions in their community of banks. Close interfamily cooperation became a cornerstone of the clans' mentality, and banking would unite the families professionally in the 20th century as clearly as had agricultural life in earlier times. In fact, throughout C.Q.'s five decades in the profession, so many sons, brothers, cousins, and nephews became involved in banking, especially in Chandler institutions, that C.Q.'s friends often accused him lightheartedly of being obliged to build his banking empire in order to accommodate his family.[3]

There was some truth in the matter, for nothing pleased Chandler more than to assist his relatives in finding a place in the industry, if such was their expressed wish. Even then, he was careful not to permit any two members of the same generation to serve simultaneously in the management of the same bank. It was his way of avoiding the consequences of competitive professional ambitions—and of stressing the importance of family solidarity and cooperation. Such a rule was not surprising, for C.Q. undoubtedly felt it was his responsibility not only to promote the professional development of the various family members but also to protect them from unneeded internal conflicts.[4]

He was equally precise in other banking practices. He felt a moral as well as a professional obligation to protect his depositors funds, and the policies he developed to fulfill that trust were products of experience and a conservative economic philosophy. Minimum expectations for his banks included sound personnel and fiscal management, adequate capital, and carefully documented and collateralized loans. To help build customer confidence in the early years, he made public a rule which forbade any officer from securing a loan from the bank he served, and it became common knowledge that he disdained long term loans on real estate because he regarded them as poor risks.[5]

He expanded his thoughts in subsequent years to embrace a variety of procedures which he expected everyone to observe— a personal and professional code so influential in the training of his associates that most of them became unrestrained devotees of his teachings. Some rules dealt with conduct within the bank, items of personal demeanor relating to image such as dress, grooming, and not smoking while at work. Others concerned the behavior of personnel within the profession itself, maxims which

A photo showing C.Q. II and a number of his banking associates, most of whom were related to each other. Included L to R: front row, Will Fallis, A.B. Masterman, E.E. Masterman, C.Q. Chandler, Paul S. Woods, Frank E. Carr; center row, Walter C. Carr, W.A. Byerley, Luther Fullerton, W.A. Lytle, C.E. Woods, H.A. Burnett; back row, J.S. Runyon, J.M. Hellings, J.W. Berryman, unknown, W.M. Price, unknown.

Frank Carson once referred to as "Chandler's Ten Rules for Success":[6]

1. A banker who takes personal advantage of information coming to him as a banker from a customer is no better than a crook.

2. If your bank can't or doesn't pay for all your time, give up your job—but don't mix your business.

3. Keep on your own side of the counter. You can't be a good lender and a heavy borrower at the same time.

4. Take an active interest in your community's affairs, but don't scatter your fire too much. Remember that your family and your church and your bank come first.

5. Be generous as the Lord has prospered you, but put your philanthropies on your expense account and not in your note case.

6. Don't waste your time trying to do business with a man whom you cannot trust; there are too many honest men with whom you can build constructively.

7. Don't be a "yes" man. Use your own judgment; stand on your own feet. I want associates, not subordinates.

8. I love to play the game. When I lose the thrill of it, I'll be ready to quit; but I don't expect to quit.

9. The big man is the one who must be ready to accept criticism. He gets it and develops under it. If he resents it, he does not get it and stagnates.

10. If you give a man a job, don't try to tell him how to do it. He develops only as he works it out himself.

A sound banking philosophy was integral to the most unique of C.Q.'s legacies—four sons, who not only shared his enthusiasm for the profession but also elected to follow careers in banking. And remarkably, Chandler's three daughters married men who also became bankers, adding even more significance to what has been called "a banking family." Thus, his professional philosophies were continued through the lives of his children and, as time would tell, his children's children.

However much he may have hoped for such a development, Chandler nonetheless was careful not to exert pressure on any of them to follow in his footsteps. He once remarked that "choosing the right profession after careful deliberation is the greatest factor toward success in life."[7] After his children had made their career choices, C.Q. felt both a fatherly and a professional obligation to see that they were properly trained. Without exception, his sons (and sons-in-law) "won their banking spurs" in the field as officials in smaller banks, just as he had done. This was especially true for Charles Jerome, his oldest son, whom C.Q. had groomed for leadership in the First National Bank.

C.J., or Charley as he was frequently called, was 43 and a vice president of FNB when his father died. Shortly thereafter, at a Board of Directors meeting on January 11, 1944, he was elected president, succeeding Frank Carson who was made Chairman of the Board. It was an expected progression of leadership and was the first major change in FNB's top officials since 1927 when Carson replaced the deceased C.W. Carey. Ironically, C.J.'s first permanent appointment as an assistant cashier of the bank occurred in 1928, a few months after Carson became president. Becoming the bank's chief operating officer had come for C.J. after 15 fortunate years of direct association with C.Q. and Carson, two of the industry's most knowledgable teachers.[8]

Even more fortunate was the fact that "all his life [C.J.] had the benefit of his father's instruction in the business." Indeed he had. During his youth, the Chandler household was like a stage upon which a master thespian tantalized a youthful and aspiring actor; as a result, a father's achievements became his son's goals. "My husband grew up," Alice Cromwell Chandler has said, "absorbing all this marvelous education just from knowing his father, and they were as close as close can be. He went to work at the bank at 12 swatting flies, and his father of course paid the money personally based on the number of flies he killed." During some summers, he served as a messenger and often accompanied bank officials when important papers were being delivered to customers. And there always was a mixture of sadness and happiness when father Chandler would insist that he spend an occasional summer at the Culver Military Academy. He enjoyed the Academy, but he was afraid he would miss some learning experience at the bank.[9]

The pattern continued after Charley entered Wichita High School—formal education in the classroom, practical experience

C.J. Chandler enjoyed many experiences because of his closeness to his father. Here he is shown with President William Howard Taft whom he drove, along with his father, from Wichita to Newton in 1919.

at the bank. He enjoyed English and history and had a special talent for public speaking. "I would work for hours on a speech," his wife remembers from a class they shared, "and he would come to class without even a note and just stand up and speak extemporaneously on anything. He had such a volume of knowledge from being with his father all the time."

Alice and C.J. shared other activities. As a staff member on the school magazine, she recognized his natural talents as a cartoonist and persuaded him to contribute humorous drawings on athletic activities. He eventually became sports editor for the publication. She even recalls that on "Freak Day," when students dressed up in silly clothes and painted their faces, he did a masterful job of emulating a circus clown, complete with facial markings of professional quality. He did not, however, share her interest in the theatre. Although he condescended occasionally to watch her perform, "he couldn't get into the make believe part of it. He'd just sit there and suffer, and would say that it was embarrassing to see all of us up there making fools of ourselves."

Charley enjoyed sports, especially basketball, but he was never tall enough to make the varsity. He also played softball and baseball, and swam at the YMCA but not competitively. Later he loved to play golf, but his work schedule left him little time to perfect his game. He also enjoyed social activities, especially after his relationship with Alice advanced from schoolmate to soulmate, but even those interests were constrained by his parents' strict behaviorial code. He was on a tight allowance because C.Q. felt his children should learn to handle their money, and he was not allowed to attend dances. Thus, most of their activities centered around other school functions and planned entertainment at home. "Charles was very obedient," Alice has said, "and respected his father's wishes. He would never do anything behind his back, not out of fear of being punished but because he didn't want to hurt his father's feelings."

True love, it has been said, always will find its way, and it did. Despite the fact that Alice was allowed to date only on Friday and Saturday evenings, and never with the same boy on successive nights, she and C.J. became acknowledged and recognized "steadies." By the time they graduated from Wichita High in May

C.J. was a member of the YMCA swimming team and is pictured third from right.

of 1921, they considered themselves engaged in an unannounced arrangement to which their parents consented—provided they both attended separate colleges. "Our parents felt it was not proper,"Alice recalls, "for engaged couples to attend the same school."[10]

C.J. had chosen for his future wife a young woman of refinement whose family background, like his, was of British extraction. Her father was Edward Joseph Cromwell (a descendant of the English family made famous by Oliver Cromwell) who began his professional career as a Methodist evangelist before permanently entering the insurance business. Her mother was Harriet Bacon, whose surname could be traced to a line of nobles bearing the title of Lord Bacon. Around the turn of the 20th century, her parents migrated to Oklahoma when it still was the Indian Territory, and since Alice was born in 1903 at Blackwell,

C.J. often made lighthearted reference to her origin by asking others: "Did you know that Alice wasn't born in the United States?" She apparently accepted his teasing as a challenge to "straighten that young man out after we are married." That opportunity, however, was several years in the future.

In the fall of 1921, Alice attended Washburn College in Topeka, and Charley went to Centre College in Danville, Kentucky, a small Presbyterian school which then admitted only men. Both attempted to become involved in campus activities, he becoming an SAE, she a Theta. However, their three years of tortured separation and loneliness were offset only by summers together in Wichita and by the excitement of a nationally visible football program coached by the legendary Bo McMillan. "For weeks," Alice remembers, "every letter I received from C.J. had 'Beat Harvard' scrolled across the outside flap, and when Centre finally defeated the Ivy League school, for months thereafter my letters bore 'Centre 6—Harvard 0' in creative, triumphant lettering on the envelopes. It was the highlight of his years at Centre."[11]

Neither graduated from college, although Charley transferred for one semester to Cumberland University in Tennessee to study business law. Alice left school a year before C.J. did, and took employment at the First National Bank in the credit department. Finally Charley convinced his father that he had learned all he could in college and that he was anxious to return to work at the bank. He joined the FNB in the summer of 1924, but was not destined to remain long.

In August, Charley went to Gage, Oklahoma, as cashier and a director of the First State Bank. C.Q. felt the situation was ideal for his son, for he believed it "the best training in the world for a young man to go into a bank in which a town had lost faith, and rebuild it." At 22, C.J. certainly was young enough; the First State Bank was in receivership when his father bought the financially troubled institution; and prior to 1924, the citizens of Gage had witnessed repeated bank failures. Thus, Charley's first major assignment was a challenge worthy of his father's most exacting specifications, but he had the Chandler reputation and his own determination to succeed as weapons in his professional arsenal.[12]

First State Bank in Gage, Oklahoma, with C.J. Chandler in cashier's cage under stuffed deer.

Equally important was the fact that by April 12, 1925, he had Alice as his inspiration and constant companion. They were married on Easter Sunday at the First Presbyterian Church in Wichita and left the same evening by automobile for their new home in Gage because Charley had to be present to open the bank on Monday morning. There was but one other employee, a young woman who had worked in the bank before it had failed. She was hired as a record keeper and had to perform her work on "an old bookkeeping machine with a one arm crank." The bank had only one bank cage and window from which Charley served as teller, loan officer, and accounts reconciler at the close of the business day. Additionally, he found time to serve as counselor to customers with financial problems, and he also swept the floors and cleaned the windows on a daily schedule which often spanned the hours from 6:00 A.M. to 10:30 P.M.[13]

Alice hardly anticipated the lifestyle she found in tiny Gage. It was a town of some 700 people which existed largely as a service center for a farming community in the Wolf Creek area of western Oklahoma. There was little or no social life, no medical facilities, and scant relief from the routine of rural life except for the periodic intrusions of Santa Fe trains as they made their way through the dusty town enroute to California. Still, Alice described their life in Gage as wonderful, and she accepted without complaint the long hours C.J. spent in rebuilding the confidence that had been lost in his bank. She managed their household on C.J.'s modest $125 per month salary, and also responded supportively, assuming responsibilites for which she had no training, when C.J.'s young female clerk suffered an acute attack of appendicitis and was forced to resign. Together they won the admiration and respect of the entire community.

On September 1, 1926, the happy couple was blessed with the arrival of their first child, a son named Charles Quarles III, whose birth assured the continuation of the direct and unbroken lineage of Richard Chandler, the first kinsman in colonial America. Because Gage had no hospital, C.J. drove Alice to Wichita a few weeks before the baby was born in order that she might receive appropriate medical attention. She and little "Chuck" rejoined him in Gage shortly after the birth.[14]

The C.J. Chandlers remained in Gage until 1928. By then, community faith in the First State Bank was fully restored, and although it was not large, the bank had become the symbol of stability for the town and its service area. Charley also was growing in professional stature and responsibilities. He developed skills in handling commercial loans, and he demonstrated an almost ingenius aptitude for managing bonds and securities, a difficult and important bank function. By January 10, 1928, he was elected President of the First State Bank, and was appointed to

Charley and Alice at home in Gage, with infant son Charles Quarles III in 1927.

the Board of Directors for banks in Higgins and Spearman, Texas; and Coats and Elkhart, Kansas. Even more impressive was the fact that he was elected to simultaneous presidencies in three of them: First State Bank of Gage; First National Bank of Higgins, Texas; and Coats State Bank of Coats, Kansas.[15]

Just when Gage was beginning to be home for the C.J. Chandlers, C.Q. summoned them to Wichita. Back-to-back deaths in 1927-28 of some key First National personnel, including President C.W. Carey, created vacancies in some critical offices, one of which was in the area of C.J.'s strongest interests. Alice remembers well the discussion which resulted in their return to Wichita. She recalls C.Q. as saying that he was sorry to bring them back since they still were quite young but that he needed Charley's skills, particularly in handling bonds. "I hate to put you in such an important and difficult area," he continued, "where you must handle a job normally done by a 45 to 50 year old man. But, you can do it."[16]

Charley resigned his presidencies and directorships and on June 30, 1928, accepted a position as Assistant Cashier and Director of the First National Bank in Wichita. He purchased a new home at 235 South Terrace Drive, and although he would make additions to the house as his family grew, it would be the only residence the family would occupy in a career which would encompass four decades at FNB. And, family expansion did come on September 16, 1930, when a second son, Jerome Lewis, was born to the Chandlers. It was obvious that they were adjusting comfortably to both home and job.[17]

Indeed, Charley quickly earned his place in the bank's officialdom. He was elected to a vice presidency on January 8, 1929, and in March, the *Wichita Beacon* recognized his return to the city in a column entitled "The Wichita Family Album," stating that he was "short of stature and of speech, but long of wisdom and easy of handshake. We predict a great future for Charley." And well they should have. In addition to his bank duties, he already had found time to become "an active member of the Blue Lodge, Royal Arch Masons, Baptist Church, Wichita Club, Sigma Alpha Epsilon Fraternity, Chamber of Commerce, Reserve City Banker, and the Kiwanis Club." In 1931, he switched his civic club membership to Rotary International, and a decade later he would be elected to serve as club president. Clearly, he had responded well to the largess of professional and civic values which he had inherited from his father.[18]

A decade of close association between C.Q. and C.J. followed his return to Wichita. Their closeness was fueled by a son's admiration and a father's devotion—and the enthusiasm both had for their profession. Like his father, C.J. worked long hours and had time for few hobbies other than reading. At the end of a workday, he sometimes walked the few blocks which separated his home from 200 South Clifton in order to enjoy a prolonged, after-hours' visit with his father. More often however, he sought seclusion with his family at home, dividing his evening hours between his children and his carefully selected library of reading materials, many of which were religious in content.[19]

Religion was important to Charley, for he spent countless hours in quiet reflection on matters of faith and in reading books on mysticism, such as Thomas á Kempis' *Imitation of Christ*. Floyd Amsden, one of his closest friends, shared his interest in the subject, and the two men enjoyed debating the finer philosophical issues on which they disagreed. C.J. had been raised as a Baptist, but because Alice was Presbyterian, and because he was very fond of her pastor, the Reverend Ray Anderson, C.J. transferred his membership from the First Baptist to the First Presbyterian Church shortly after returning to Wichita. The change was fully discussed with C.Q. who not only respected his son's decision but also thought it appropriate since it united the young family in worship.[20]

Charley took his responsibilities seriously and became a leader in the church, initiating in later years a monthly meditation session where men could gather and sit in spiritual silence before going to work. The men did not posture these meetings as just another worship service; indeed, brief readings delivered occasionally by the participants focused on moral and ethical teachings found in secular literature. Yet, their experiences were powerful and uplifting and drew active businessmen closer together in their professional relationships.[21]

Increasingly, C.J.'s leadership abilities were utilized in other areas. In 1933, he became the youngest person in the United States to head a Community Chest drive, and during his presidency, the Wichita Chest enjoyed the most successful fund drive in its history. In the same year he was appointed to membership on the Tenth District Federal Deposit Liquidation Committee whose duty it was to appraise the assets of Kansas banks which had closed and which were applying for federal liquidation aid. He was elected in 1935 as a vice president of the American Bankers Association for Kansas, and was honored by being listed in

Charles Jerome Chandler as a young, rising banker in Wichita.

"Who's Who in Banking" in the May 15, 1935, edition of *Bank News*. Then in 1940, the Kansas Society for Crippled Children chose him as second vice president of the organization which his father had headed since its formation in 1929.[22]

All of these experiences were important milestones along a road which led inevitably to the greater role he would play in family, bank, and civic affairs following C.Q.'s death in late December of 1943. In the short span of a few months, C.J. became the executor of his father's estate, president of the First National Bank, and president of the Kansas Society for Crippled Children. Moreover, as the oldest son, he assumed surrogate responsibilities for the clan, including the financial management of the Chandler Trust.[23]

Fortunately, by the time C.J. became president of the First National in 1944, the worst effects of the Great Depression had passed, but the nation was in the midst of a different type of crisis: a global war in which Charley's oldest son, Chuck, as well as his two youngest brothers, George and Anderson, were involved as servicemen. To do his part in the war effort, C.J. joined a committee of distinguished Wichitans, which included E.B. Shawver, Walter P. Innis, Paul Jernigan, Frank L. Carson, W.B. Harrison, Arthur W. Kincade, Sam Wallingford, and Steve Wise, and helped spearhead a successful bond drive in Sedgwick County to raise money which was needed to finance the conflict. The *Wichita Beacon* paid him special tribute in July of 1945 along with other "worthwhile leaders" such as wartime generals Douglas MacArthur, Carl Spaatz, and Curtis LeMay.[24]

Such service became characteristic of C.J.'s commitment to his city. Almost every major community project thereafter would find his name listed among other civic minded citizens who sought to improve the quality of life in Wichita and Sedgwick County. Gordon Evans, longtime chief executive of the Kansas Gas and Electric Company in Wichita and a perennial fund raiser for numerous causes, remembers that he never "went over to him for money for any civic purpose that he didn't support, even when he had no personal attachment to the activity." For example, Evans continued, "he didn't have a particularly strong interest in the symphony, but he thought Wichita ought to have one and

*War Bond Drive Committee in 1942, showing Frank Carson seated first
on left, and C.J. Chandler standing first on right.*

thus deserved his support. He always gave personally, and saw
to it that contributions also were made by the bank." Moreover,
it became a tradition for a liberal sprinkling of bank personnel,
both officers and employees, to take leadership roles in all civic
and philanthropic organizations in Wichita—without thought of
personal compensation.[25]

In the two decades following World War II, C.J. and Frank
Carson led the First National into a new era of banking service
for its customers. Indeed, the entire area of customer service
and relations had to be redefined to complement a modern continuum which elevated consumer credit to the top of the bank's
planning agenda. Increased postwar demands by the average
citizen set off what has been called "the consumer revolution,"
the earliest facet of which was an insistence upon immediate possession or consumption of goods and services supported by installment credit. Loan policies in previous years had followed
C.Q.'s precedents, targeting business and industry as principal
clients and dealing conservatively with small, personal transac-

tions. Although there was no wholesale departure from past traditions, the speed with which the bank recognized and moved to accommodate the new trend testifies to the importance Carson and Chandler placed on it.[26]

The decision was made in 1945 to establish a consumer loan department, and an aggressive program of advertising and public relations was initiated to attract new customers. Paul Harlow Woods, who had just returned from Army service, was assigned to head the new effort, a wise choice for the bank and an excellent opportunity for another resourceful member of the Chandler-Woods-Berryman banking family. Still, it was an inervating undertaking. Since FNB officials were unable to predict the longterm effects of the action, they were, as Woods has said, required in the beginning to "keep one foot in the past and one in the future." The subsequent successes from their efforts more than offset early fears.[27]

That program was but one of the innovations C.J. authorized in his attempt to attract a larger volume of smaller accounts and to render more efficient service to bank patrons. In 1952, he announced plans for the construction of a new drive-in bank facility, stating that the new addition was a continuation of a "long established policy of this bank in providing the most up-to-date equipment and facilities possible in order to render the maximum of service ... for our many customers, who now find it necessary to park in order to transact their banking business." The bank-by-auto service became operational on August 10, 1953, when Mayor Walt Keeler drove up to one of the four cashiers' windows and, amid flashing cameras, made the first deposit.[28]

Regular banking customers were not neglected. In 1955, a spacious parking lot was completed at Douglas and Water, and in a carefully worded news release in July of the following year, C.J. outlined plans for the construction of a new two-story addition to the original 1921 structure which would house, among other functions, First National's Personal Loan Department. Designed by Forsblom and Parks, Architects, and completed in May of 1958 by the Martin K. Eby Construction Company at a cost of $650,000, the 6000 square foot expansion tastefully complemented the older building and extended the bank's lobby "a full

Wichita Mayor Walt Keeler, shown here with C.J. Chandler (first on left), makes first deposit at FNB's new drive-in teller.

half block west." It provided, according to the bank's proud president, sufficient space "to fully accommodate our present customers and ensure ample facilities for many more years of growth in Wichita."[29]

Several years before the opening of the expanded facility, the First National had been saddened by the death of Frank Carson who had served as Chairman of the Board since 1944. However, following the tradition set by C.Q. Chandler, Carson and C.J. had prepared for the transition in leadership by systematically identifing and carefully preparing a cadre of talented associates who could provide continuity to the management of the bank. Heading the list in 1958 was Paul Harlow Woods, by then executive vice president, whose connection with the First National had begun in 1928.[30]

Woods' father, Paul Scott Woods, also was a former Chandler associate, having left a South Dakota bank position in 1899 to join C.Q. when he purchased the Farmers and Stockgrowers Bank of Ashland. The elder Woods then was sent to help organize the Liberal State Bank, but later moved to Kingman where he became part owner of the First National Bank, another of Chandler's "community of banks." There he met and married Grace Harlow, and young Paul, who was born in 1906, grew up "knowing his way around the bank." He attended the University of Kansas where he became an outstanding athlete, and after earning his B.S. degree in Business Administration he was offered a coaching job in a small eastern Kansas high school, a job which would have paid him three times the salary he received in the job he finally accepted—at the First National Bank in Wichita where he later would become president.[31]

After a month in Wichita, Woods briefly became an itinerant banker, spending short stints in both Gage, Oklahoma (where C.J. was president), and Perryton, Texas, before returning to Wichita in 1928. When his father became seriously ill in 1929, he moved to Kingman and accepted an assistant cashier's position in his father's bank in order to help and be near him until he died. Paul remained in Kingman from 1929 until 1934, during which time he married Wilda Cline, a former high school classmate. He then accepted an assignment with the Federal Intermediate Credit Bank in Wichita, serving as secretary and as a member of the FICB executive committee until 1938 when he was appointed to "a specially created office of assistant vice president" in the correspondent banking program at the First National Bank. Thereafter, his tenure at FNB was interrupted only by his service as an Army finance officer during World War II.[32]

Paul was in the forefront of the bank's innovations after 1945, serving directly with C.J. in shaping many of the First National's new programs. The substance of a shared ancestry, mutual admiration, and personal respect developed over many years formed a strong bond between them, but Woods' promotions were earned by his professional performances. Thus, another natural progression in FNB leadership, similar to the one in January of 1944, occurred on June 10, 1958, when Charles Jerome Chandler became Chairman of the Board and Paul Woods replaced him as President. Not to be overlooked in these Board actions which

Paul Harlow Woods, President of First National, and his wife Wilda.

named the chief officers of the bank was the appointment of Charles Quarles Chandler III, C.J.'s oldest son, to an executive vice presidency, an action which reflected the professional growth of a younger member of the clan and which set the stage for yet another natural progression in the future.[33]

Continuity in leadership, it has been said, may have been the First National's greatest asset over the years. At no time since the bank was purchased in 1900 has it been without a Chandler at the helm, either as chairman of the board or president, or both. Equally as important is the fact that each of the Chandlers has been guided by good instincts in personnel selection, to the end that men of commanding personality and outstanding ability—

In 1958, C.J. Chandler became Chairman of the Board, Paul Woods became President, and C.Q. Chandler III became Executive Vice President of FNB.

a Frank Carson or a Paul Woods—always are prepared to share in the bank's executive leadership.

C.J., a basic conservative, and Paul, an admitted progressive, complemented each other well in the era of expanding bank services. They moved cautiously in some areas, such as expanding time deposits, and relentlessly in others, as in aggressively soliciting dealer paper in order to increase the bank's installment loan business. An expensive program in the early 1960s led to the automation of bank services, a pioneering effort among Wichita banks which greatly accelerated FNB's volume of daily transactions, not only from normal customer traffic but also from sharing computer time with smaller financial institutions in the area.

Perhaps the most important spinoff from the automation of services was that it facilitated the emergence of "the age of plastics"—a bank credit card system which made instant credit available to almost every account holder in the bank. In 1968, the Chandler-Woods team chose Master Charge as the medium through which it would expand such service, and a sizeable number of retail stores was persuaded to join in the three-cornered system of providing consumer credit at the point of sales. The result has been an explosion of small loans for an almost limitless variety of goods and services—and a dramatic increase in bank revenues.[35]

Woods' progressive spirit also left its impact upon employment policies. A person who believes strongly in human rights and equality of opportunity, Paul was an advocate of hiring minorities, especially women, as bank officers long before it became an impassioned political subject or a legal consideration. With C.J.'s full support, he helped identify and recruit such women as Lillian Burke, Peggy Wesley, and Dorothy Ray who became career bankers and officers in FNB. Lillian served as an assistant cashier until her death in 1965; Peggy rose to become the bank's customer service officer, a position she now has held for a decade; and Dorothy currently is senior vice president of the Investment Division and is the highest ranking female officer at FNB. Their professional achievements and Woods' persistence encouraged an early progressive attitude toward the development of a diversified staff based on ability.[35]

As the decade of the 1970's approached, the bank's principal policy architects in the post World War II era were nearing the end of their careers, but neither C.J. nor Paul showed visible signs of slowing their pace. To support the growth they had initiated and, hopefully, to sustain its momentum, a program of plant modernization was undertaken in 1968. A high-rise parking garage, connected to the main building by stairwells and elevators, was constructed, and the remaining strip of property fronting Douglas Avenue was beautifully landscaped, complete with a pool and fountain. Additionally, the older portions of the bank building were renovated and redecorated "without interfering with the artistic integrity of the original design." Fortunately, all of the changes were made before the costs of construction soared to almost prohibitive levels in later years.[36]

On July 14, 1971, Paul Woods announced his retirement as president, and effective on August 1, C.Q. "Chuck"Chandler III at age 45 was elected to succeed him. For a short time, a father-son combination directed the bank, but declining health limited C.J.'s activities during the ensuing months. Finally, in 1974 his stamina waned noticeably, and following a brief illness and confinement at his home at 235 South Terrace Drive, he passed away on Sunday, December 15. Shortly thereafter, Chuck assumed his father's role as chairman of the board while retaining the title of president as well.[37]

A summary of C.J.'s achievements, published on December 16, 1974, in the *Wichita Eagle*, left no doubt as to the significance of the life just ended. As a professional banker, he had been honored by being asked to serve in various leadership roles for city, state, and national organizations, such as the Reserve City Bankers, the Kansas Bankers, and the American Bankers associations. Further recognition came in 1953 when he was appointed to the Federal Advisory Council to the Board of Governors for the Federal Reserve System, an important assignment which took him quarterly to Washington as a respesentative of the Tenth Federal Reserve District in Kansas City. And, in 1967 he was presented with a commemorative medal by Congress "in recognition of [his] leadership and contributions to the agriculture industry."

His civic participation over the years was equally as impressive. In addition to his service in the Wichita Rotary Club and the Kansas Society for Crippled Children, he had been active on the Kansas Gas and Electric Company Board of Directors, the University of Wichita (now Wichita State University) Development Board, the Ottawa University Board of Trustees, the Quivira Scout Council, and the National Conference of Christians and Jews, an organization which in 1966 presented him with its coveted Brotherhood Award in recognition "for lifetime service to the

After Paul Woods retired in 1971, a father-son combination directed the First National Bank in Wichita.

community." C.J. also was involved in a number of "firsts" for Wichita. In 1952 he was named as the city's first jury commissioner and helped supervise the selection of juries not only in Wichita but also in Hutchinson and Dodge City. Additionally, he was the founder of Junior Achievement in the city, and was one of the organizers of the Wichita United Fund.[38]

Thus had the *Eagle's* obituary assigned Charles Jerome Chandler's accomplishments to the ledger containing the accumulated record of his family's rich past which, by his father's definition, now became prologue for those who came after him. As a man of faith, C.J. clearly understood the analogy between his inheritance and the biblical parable on the stewardship of talents. The option of burying his "talents" was one he never entertained; indeed, he was too much like his father in personal philosophy and professional commitments to have considered any course other than the one he followed—that of leading the First National to new goals along fresh frontiers of service. By the time of his death, bank patrons and professional colleagues spoke of his achievements with the same expressions of admiration and respect they had used in evaluating those of his father.

Chandler was a calm, businesslike person who expressed his opinions in a manner so sensible that no one felt he was trying to impose his judgment on them. He had a reputation of being very approachable, and his office was always open to those who wanted to see him. Gordon Evans remembers that many individuals went to him for counseling, but that it was not in his nature to "go around telling people what to do" or to volunteer advice without being asked. Even when asked, C.J. merely offered the options he perceived and allowed people to decide issues for themselves. "They came to him," Evans believes, "because people knew that he was a man of high integrity and strong character who had no axes to grind—that his only interest was in seeing that things came out right."[39]

Evans felt C.J.'s contributions on the Kansas Gas and Electric Board of Directors were outstanding in that regard. "He was very free in stating his opinions in a businesslike and sensible manner, and when things didn't go just right, he could be very encouraging in his calm, dignified way. He would tell us that we should expect plateaus in our business experiences because it was impossible to set new records every year. 'Life,' he would say, 'is just not like that'."

According to Gordon Evans' assessment, C.J. "was a sound

businessman, conservative in the sense that he didn't want to see things get out of hand, yet progressive in the sense that he wanted to see things improve— not just financially but also from the standpoint of the quality of life. He had no sense of greed or power, and had little flair about him. Charley was a loyal friend and thoroughly enjoyed the company of such men as Wash Lilleston with whom he shared many happy hours. He was one of the few men I have known whom I considered absolutely honest, both intellectually and morally. He would never speak uncomplimentary about anyone. If ever there was a question about a person's integrity, the worst thing he ever would say was, 'Well, he's just not our kind of people'."[40]

To some, such a statement might have implied veiled snobbery, but not to those who knew C.J. well. "There was no stuffiness and not an ounce of vanity in the man," Paul Woods avows; "I never worked for a fellow who was any nicer or who treated me with greater kindness than Charley. He was a man of great compassion, and sort of laid back and low keyed all the time. He was chairman of the board of a bank owned largely by his family and could have done just about anything he wanted to do, but he trusted and deferred to my judgment on many of the policy changes we made together over the years—sometimes not as rapidly as I thought necessary but always with his complete support. He respected his competitors, especially Arthur Kincade over at Fourth National whom he had met when both of them were first starting out in the business. Charley was at Gage [Oklahoma], Arthur at a small bank in Texas, and it was sheer irony that both would wind up in Wichita in rival institutions, but they always got along very well."[41]

Despite the long hours he worked at the bank, C.J. was not one to put business above family. The Chandlers lived comfortably in their South Terrace Drive home, but were not given to extravagance nor were they involved in extensive social activities. They held membership in the Wichita Country Club, frequently dining there with friends on weekends, and Charley occasionally played a round of golf, more (it is said) for sport than for score. Alice and C.J. rarely attended other club functions and were not bridge players, but they sometimes held

C.J. was proud of his family. Shown here are C.Q. III and Georgia; C.J. and Alice; and Jerome and Lois, at the Innes Tea Room in 1952.

"grudge matches" in games such as Monopoly with their sons at home. Their children largely were under Alice's supervision, and she recalls having played "just about every game there is" with her two sons and their friends, in sessions that often lasted well into the late evening hours. Chuck and Jerome were required to observe normal social hours and activities, and they were kept on a strict allowance. The Chandler household was a balanced, orderly, and happy environment, made so because C.J. and Alice placed great emphasis on family development and unity. It was a part of the Chandler tradition.[42]

An extension of the same heritage was the respect C.J. had for his brothers and sisters. All of them, three brothers and three sisters with birthdates ranging from 1901 to 1926, had fond memories of the happy home in which they had grown up, memories which formed the strongest of bonds between them as young adults. In later years, a common profession added another enduring dimension to their relationships. Tightly knit as kinsmen, they took delight in being referred to as "a banking family."

6

A FAMILY OF BANKERS:
C.Q.'s EARLIER CHILDREN

As hard as it is for an entrepreneur to make a success of a business he has started or, for that matter, to build onto the achievements of one he has purchased from a previous owner, it is even more difficult to inherit a firm and maintain the image and momentum associated with a long-tenured and highly-successful relative. In short, C.Q. Chandler II was "a hard act to follow," not only for Charles Jerome but also for the other six brothers and sisters once they became a part of the family of bankers. Although his outstanding record became the benchmark by which the financial community measured his children's accomplishments, none of the younger Chandlers has used that yardstick in setting personal or professional goals. Each of them has drawn liberally upon C.Q.'s legacy, but each has travelled a road in the financial world which seemed most appropriate to them, given their individual personalities, interests, and abilities. Each has been a competitor only with himself.

Certainly C.J. did not regard himself as being in competition with the memory of his father's accomplishments; indeed, he seemed almost apologetic at times for being C.Q.'s oldest son, and thus for having been given the excellent opportunity to rise first in the management of the Chandler banks. C.J. was driven by his own pride to succeed in his own way, for he knew that his father, as much as he revered him and brilliant a teacher though he was, could not return from his grave to correct his errors. "Failure," C.J. was fond of saying, "is an orphan, but success has many fathers."[1]

His brothers and sisters—Margaret (born in 1901), William (1904), Elizabeth (1906), Olive (1919), George (1921), and Anderson (1926)—were of the same mind: the past was indeed but

Margaret (first on right) is shown with her brothers and sister in 1911 before her illness.

prologue. All were a part of a rich family heritage, but an essential part of that inheritance was the knowledge that they had personal responsibilities for their own destinies. The warmth and respect they held for each other was as enviable as the independence each asserted was understandable.[2]

None of them gained wider respect for struggling against life's complexities than Margaret. As a young girl, she fell victim to infantile paralysis, a frightening disease which totally paralyzed one leg and partially the other. Even though she was fortunate to have parents wealthy enough to care for all her medical and personal needs, the trauma of facing the future as a cripple was intense. To one so young, the easiest course would have been to view her dilemma with bitterness and "curse the fates." Instead, she summoned inner strength and embarked on a lifetime battle against her affliction, undergoing more than 30 operations and scores of brace fittings until she all but conquered the immobilizing effects of her illness. In the process, her courage and partial recovery inspired her father to initiate a benevolent crippled children's movement which extended hope and relief to literally thousands of youths in Kansas.[3]

Her courage also allowed her to enjoy a full and happy life, not without incoveniences but certainly without pity. Older than Charles by a year, Margaret always assumed the role of "big sister" in the Chandler home and insisted upon sharing household responsibilities even when her crutches and braces made them burdensome. She refused, politely in all cases, to let anyone "make on over her," preferring to do as many things for herself as possible when she was bedridden following one of her frequent operations. "She was as sweet as sweet can be," Elizabeth, her younger sister, remembers; "everyone just loved her because she refused to succumb to despair."[4]

Margaret received most of her early education at home, tutored along with her brothers and sister in a space her father added as a sleeping porch adjoining the bedroom she shared with Elizabeth. All four of the earlier children transferred to College Hill School, a public institution, after Alice became mistress of the Chandler household because their new mother was a former teacher and felt they should have public school associations and experiences. For a brief time, Margaret was persuaded by her minister's daughter, Kathleen Smith, to attend Virginia Intermont School in Bristol, Virginia, for a school year. Later, she graduated from Wichita High school, and moved to live with an uncle in Emporia where she attended and graduated in 1924 from Emporia State Teachers College.

By then, Margaret had mastered her afflictions and had learned to walk reasonably well with the aid of leg braces, an achievement which served as an inspiration to "hundreds of little children [who] hobble on twisted little legs." She engaged "in the normal activities of other young women" and even drove her own car. She was active in the First Baptist Church and taught Sunday School for a few years. There she met and fell in love with Kenneth Braley who operated a service station in west Wichita. She

Margaret, who inspired her father to develop the crippled children's move-ment in Kansas, is shown (fifth from left) with the directors of the Kansas Society for Crippled Children in July of 1931.

was teased unmercifully about the fact that she often drove "clear across town" to get gasoline, but she took the ribbing in stride. Eventually, through contacts with the family, Braley asked for an opportunity to learn the banking business, and C.Q. arranged for him to go to Holly, Colorado, as an assistant cashier.[5]

For two years, Margaret and Kenneth traded visits, she spending long weekends at the home of her uncle, Edward J. Thayer, who once had run the First National Bank of Holly. Their engagement was announced on April 7, 1935, and following a round of bridal showers, they were married on April 25 at the First Baptist Church, after which they departed immediately for a new home in Holly which Alice had helped in preparing and appointing. The couple enjoyed four happy years in tiny Holly. Grace Elizabeth, their only child, was born on November 26, 1936, and Kenneth promptly earned his place in "the family of bankers." By 1938, he had become the managing officer of the First National in Holly.[6]

In the last months of 1938, Braley began to look for a bank of his own. With C.Q.'s help, he investigated a number of possibil-

Margaret and Kenneth G. Braley on their wedding day.

The Braley family in 1952, L to R: Grace Elizabeth, Kenneth, Margaret.

ities and finally focussed on the Farmers Exchange Bank in Cherokee, Oklahoma. On January 17, 1939, Peter Stein, owner of the bank, revealed that he had sold controlling interests in the bank to "Kenneth Braley and associates." The stockholders, he announced, had elected K.G. Braley as president and Paul H. Woods of Wichita as a new director. The move to Cherokee was permanent for Margaret and Kenneth, and the Chandler heritage was extended to yet another western Oklahoma community. Margaret died in 1955; Braley ultimately sold his bank and retired in Cherokee.[7]

Margaret maintained close contact with the other members of her family, one of whom, William Woods Chandler, already had become vice president and chief operating officer of the Chandler National Bank in Lyons, Kansas, a year before her marriage to Kenneth. Billy (as he was called in his youth) got to Lyons along a route as circuitous as any that was travelled by a Chandler in reaching a permanent location. Moreover, some evidence exists which indicates that banking was not his first career choice even though he had received the same exposure his older brother Charley had during their formative years.

Billy's early educational experiences were like those of Margaret and C.J.: tutoring at home until 1917, after which he attended College Hill School and Wichita High School. As a youth,

Meeting at Farmers Exchange Bank in Cherokee, Oklahoma, in 1950. Pictured L to R: seated, T.C. Peffer, Robert M. Clogston, Kenneth G. Braley, M.C. Mason, Paul H. Woods; standing, W.W. Chandler, Jr., George T. Chandler, Arthur Lane, C.J. Chandler, Anderson W. Chandler, Carl Dunnington, Clark Dunnington, J.R. Pate, C.Q. Chandler III, Ray Geist.

he was a spirited lad with an outgoing personality. He enjoyed outdoor activities and was especially fond of hunting and "going to car races." Much earlier than the other children, he asserted an independence which frustrated his father, but it was difficult to be overly harsh with a youngster whose rebellious antics were more precocious than defiant. He loved playing with firecrackers and almost always carried a few of them in his coat pockets. Unsuspecting playmates (and family members) frequently were "treated to a surprise or two" during a relaxing activity. Additionally, he often would spend long afternoons hunting rattlesnakes and prairie dogs and return home with the obvious smell of cigarette smoke in his clothing, but he always managed to survive his parents' remonstrations.[8]

After graduating from high school, father C.Q. urged him to

*Billy Chandler, a
spirited lad, is shown
here on right with older
brother Charley in
1906 wearing their
first hats.*

join Charley in 1923 at Centre College where he pledged SAE
and joined heartily into the various campus activities. During his
freshman year, he met "a lovely and super sweet" young lady,
Thelma Gillespie, whom he married on August 28, 1926, following a two year courtship. With his father's approval and delight, Billy made the first of his career decisions and entered the
Southern Baptist Theological Seminary in Louisville, Kentucky,
to study for the ministry.[9]

He enjoyed a productive year in Louisville, but Billy and his
young wife slowly determined that their interests in the ministry

were not strong enough to encourage them to continue. Then, when their first son, William Woods, Jr., was born on November 26, 1927, Billy decided to forego the balance of his training and become a banker like his father and brother before him. His first permanent assignment, as an assistant cashier of the First State Bank in Gage, Oklahoma, came in July of 1928 when father C.Q. brought Charley back to the First National in Wichita.[10]

The William Chandlers remained less than a year in Gage. His Uncle Ed Thayer, longtime cashier of the First National Bank of Holly, Colorado, had expressed the desire to retire, and Billy was elected on June 13, 1929, to replace him. Three months later, his responsibilities were increased when the city's other financial insitution, the Holly State Bank, was purchased by the Chandlers and consolidated with the First National. The purchase preceded only by a few weeks the collapse of the stock market and the beginning of the Great Depression.[11]

Tiny Holly became a difficult training ground for the new cashier. Bank failures were almost epidemic, and dust bowl conditions made life unbearable at times. There were not many opportunities to make good loans and little else to do but try to collect older ones from patrons who had no income. However, Billy had an infectious personality which exuded confidence, and he managed, with conservative banking practices and much advice from his father and Uncle Ed Thayer, to keep the First National solvent. For pasttime, he "shot a lot of rattlesnakes" in that parched and windwept environment, but he learned to love the town and its people. His active participation in community activities won him widespread respect, as evidenced by his election in 1930 "to the office of elder" in the First Presbyterian Church of Holly.[12]

Good things happened to Thelma and Billy during their four-plus years in Holly. They enjoyed a comfortable home among "some of the world's most friendly and hospitable people," and Thelma bore three additional children: James Jerome on August 3, 1929; Alice Catharine on February 1, 1931; and Alfred Arthur on February 15, 1932. And, Billy grew in stature, maturing by 1934 to the point where he felt prepared to accept a more demanding challenge, preferably one nearer Wichita. The

Billy and Thelma Chandler at home in Lyons, Kansas, with their family,
L to R: seated, Alice Catharine, Arthur; standing, Jim, Bill, Jr.

right opportunity came when the Lyons National Bank failed to
reopen after the bank moratorium in March of 1933, leaving the
county seat of Rice County without a financial institution. It was
a training ground of the same exacting standards into which a
younger Charles Jerome had gone a decade earlier at Gage in
western Oklahoma—and an even younger Charles Quarles
Chandler II had gone 60 years before at Elk City on the Kansas
frontier.[13]

A new charter was secured, and banking operations resumed
in the old building on March 12, 1934, under a new name—the
Chandler National Bank. Seventy-year old C.Q. became chairman of the board and president of CNB, and William Woods
Chandler at 30 was elected vice president and cashier. Those who
attended the grand opening on Monday, March 12, included a
liberal sprinkling of family and officials of the First National Bank
in Wichita, their presence helping to usher in, the *Lyons Daily
News* reported, "an era of optimism and confidence. A spirit of
good feelings was evident around the [city] square this morning."[14]

The early days of the Chandler National Bank were difficult, as they were for all small town banks. A failing national economy and a paralyzing regional drought virtually halted all but the most essential banking services, and a rash of bank holdups made even the protection of modest deposits and cash reserves perilous. The Chandler National suffered one robbery, during which Billy was taken hostage. The thieves bound his hands and feet, and as they fled the city, they threw him from the car into a ditch. Fortunately, Billy was unharmed, and the felons were swiftly apprehended and brought to justice.[15]

Lyons hardly had the volume of business activities that many of the other western Kansas towns had, but Billy was satisfied with his newfound home and resisted numerous opportunities to move after proving he could handle the difficult situation he had undertaken. The Chandler National became a symbol of hope for returning prosperity to Lyons, and the young chief operating officer's active participation in community functions endeared him the citizenry. "Billy certainly was a community leader," a family member has said, "no question about it. He was a pillar in the Presbyterian Church, and was very active in Boy Scouts and Girl Scouts." George Chandler, who idolized his brother, surmises that Billy's contentment derived from "a special set of counters" by which he lived—a personal reward structure which reflected what he thought was most important in life. Lyons offered him "just the right environment to be fully and completely himself."[16]

For over forty years, Billy Chandler ran a sound bank, for some much too conservatively, but nonetheless a very safe bank. Deposits in the Chandler National remained relatively static during the last decade of his leadership. To those who knew him best, such a record was not surprising, for "his priorities were more attuned to the community and the operation of a good, conservative bank in which the townsmen had confidence." Equally as obvious was that Billy was a disciple of C.Q.'s teachings, for "he ran the same kind of bank that he felt should be run were his father alive."[17]

Not even the establishment of a competitor bank in Lyons could cause him to change his philosophies. He was not an aggressive,

*Board of Directors of the Chandler National Bank in Lyons, L to R: seated,
B.K. Babcock, W.W. Chandler, W.W. Chandler, Jr., A.A. Chandler;
standing, Homer D. Sharpe, Cecil Bill Miller, Jerome Chandler, George
Chandler, Chuck Chandler, Ansel Tobias.*

pushy businessman, and it was not uncommon for him to pass
up loan opportunities when they failed to meet the rules he set
for his bank. However, he sometimes would risk his own funds
by carrying, in his personal note case, the financial paperwork
covering a project he believed in but which did not meet bank
standards. Then, if such a loan proved to be a bad debt, he had
to answer only to himself. His cardinal rule was never to compromise established bank policies, a procedure which was gratifying to his directors and appreciated by his depositors.

William and Thelma Chandler lived long and productive lives
in Lyons, (she until 1977, he until 1979) and were regarded as
"a virtual institution in themselves" by the people in the area.
Billy was active as a director in many of the so-called Chandler
institutions, and he oftentimes served as a consultant and trou-

Billy and Thelma Chandler in the 1970's.

ble shooter when any of them faced momentary crises. Evidence of the respect with which he was held in financial circles is the fact that he was honored by his colleagues in 1952 by being elected to serve as president of the Kansas Bankers Association, an honor which had been accorded to his father in 1900 and one which later would come to his youngest brother, Anderson Woods Chandler. And, two of Billy's sons have joined the procession of Chandlers in banking; Billy, Jr., was president of the Lyons bank prior to his death in 1980, and James Jerome, currently serves as vice president of the First National Bank of Ottawa, his Uncle Robert M. Clogston's bank.[18]

Bob Clogston's name was added to the Chandler genealogy through his marriage to Elizabeth Jean Chandler, the last of C.Q.'s earlier children. They had met while both were students at the College of Emporia. Bob received his degree in Business Administration in 1927 and spent 18 months as an employee in Chandler banks in Colorado and Texas before he persuaded Elizabeth, still two years away from her own graduation, to become his wife.

Elizabeth had matriculated at the College of Emporia because

Elizabeth Chandler standing in front of brothers Bill and Charley and sister Margaret in 1911.

"it was as far away from home as father Chandler would allow her to go" and because Margaret also was a student in the same city at Emporia State Teachers College. Prior to that time, the two sisters had shared many of the same educational experiences (though at different grade levels), including home tutoring and at College Hill and Wichita High schools. Elizabeth also attended Stephens College in Columbia, Missouri, during her high school sophomore year, but left the school to join Margaret when she went to Virginia Intermont in Bristol. However, illness forced her to return home before the year ended, and Elizabeth's par-

*Elizabeth shortly before
her marriage to Robert M.
Clogston.*

ents enrolled her at Mt. Carmel High, a private boarding school in Wichita, from which she would graduate in 1925.[19]

At the College of Emporia, Elizabeth pursued a general liberal arts program and met Clogston there during her freshman year. Bob was born in Eureka, Kansas, on April 28, 1905, to Methodist parents, Mr. and Mrs. Robert M. Clogston, Sr. The senior Clogston, a lawyer, moved to Wichita in the early 1920's, but sent his son to live with an uncle in Emporia where he enrolled in the Presbyterian-related college. Although his romance with Elizabeth became serious, her parents thought her too young to consider marriage. However, C.Q. Chandler had grown quite fond of young Bob and offered him, upon graduation in 1927, the opportunity to learn the banking business at one of his favorite training institutions— the First National Bank of Holly, Colorado.

Thus, Bob went to Holly, and Elizabeth returned to Emporia. Absence, in their case, did make the heart grow fonder, although separation made their existence miserable. Whenever she could, Elizabeth spent long weekends with her Uncle Ed Thayer in Holly in order to be near Bob, but her schoolwork limited the number of such visits. Then in the summer of 1928, Bob was transferred to Spearman, Texas, adding additional miles and complications to their visitations, and by the time Elizabeth returned to the College of Emporia for the fall semester, they could stand their separation no longer. She left school, married Bob on October 27, 1928, in a quiet ceremony at the First Baptist Church, and the couple left immediately for their new home in Spearman.[20]

Father Chandler left them in Texas for only two years, then in 1930 transferred them to the First State Bank in Elkhart, in the far southwest corner of Kansas. Depression and dust bowl conditions made professional activities difficult, and the death of an infant son on May 27, 1932, one day after his birth, added a deep sadness to their personal lives. Bob was patient, however, working hard and learning much about operating a small bank in an agrarian community. By 1936, he was ready and eager to take on larger responsibilities. A grand opportunity arose when the First National Bank of Ottawa, one of the oldest in the state, was made available to the Chandler interests.[21]

The Ottawa bank, established in 1870, ranks second only to the one in Leavenworth as being the oldest nationally chartered Kansas bank in continuous existence bearing the title of First National Bank. Frank J. Miller, its longtime and much beloved president, had died in November of 1934, after which a family member, Mrs. L.B. Miller, served as head of the bank until conditions urged her to take a less active role in its management. On May 1, 1936, she announced that "R.M. Clogston, son-in-law of C.Q. Chandler, well known banker of Wichita," had purchased "a substantial interest" in the bank, and that Clogston would become president effective immediately. Mrs. Miller continued as a member of the board of directors.[22]

The *Ottawa Herald* hailed the purchase as "Ottawa's good fortune," and happily welcomed the new owner to the city's banking and business family. The editor pointed with pride to "Mr. Clogston's personal qualifications and fine personality, and his connection with Mr. [C.Q.] Chandler [who is] one the most widely known bankers in this section of the country." Indeed, the *Herald* continued, the Wichita banker "is a longtime friend and sup-

*Elizabeth, with daughter Ann
Elizabeth and C.Q. II, at
home in Ottawa in 1937.*

porter of Ottawa University ... and Ottawans feel that he belongs
to Ottawa almost as much as he does to Wichita."[23]

After nine years with other Chandler banks, Robert and Elizabeth Clogston returned to familiar grounds. Bob was a native
of not-too-distant Eureka, and the couple had met in nearby Emporia—to them it was like going home again. They purchased
and renovated a lovely house in Ottawa, and once they took possession of it, they have never considered moving to another location, either within the city or away from Ottawa. It was a happy
home, made so by happy people and the arrival on October 24,
1936, of a daughter, Ann Elizabeth, who would be their only
child.[24]

Ottawans quickly found the Clogstons to be community leaders and willing participants in every civic activity. Like his father-
in-law before him, Bob became a strong supporter and a member of the board of trustees for Ottawa University, even though
it meant changing his church membership. He had been raised
in the Methodist Church and was a graduate of the College of
Emporia, which was Presbyterian affiliated. Ottawa University
was supported by the Baptist Church, and C.Q., who had been
made a life member of the board, convinced Bob that he should
become a trustee. Moreover, it is said, his father-in-law further

The Robert M. Clogston family, L to R: Elizabeth, Ann Elizabeth, Robert.

convinced him that all trustees should be Baptists. Clogston embraced the Baptist faith but did so, in all likelihood, because it was Elizabeth's church preference more than from any pressure he felt from Chandler. He believed that his family should share a common religious commitment and experience.[25]

Bob enjoyed a fine relationship with C.Q. and the other Chandler children. He often was asked by his father-in-law to share automobile trips, and he no doubt was extended opportunities to serve on various bank boards because C.Q. had a high regard for his banking acumen. He and Elizabeth frequently exchanged visits with the families of her brothers and sisters, although they have kept such contacts in perspective by allowing all of them the independence needed to develop their lives free of family interference. Now in her seventies, Elizabeth remains, in the 1980s, the anchor and only surviving member of C.Q.'s earlier children, and she and her husband still lead full lives and give vigorous leadership to the First National Bank of Ottawa.[26]

Thus, the four earlier Chandler children have contributed much to the legacy of "a family of bankers"—as have the three later children born to C.Q. and Alice Chandler after their mar-

Elizabeth and Bob remain active in Ottawa civic and business affairs.

riage in 1917. Elizabeth was 13 when Olive, the first of the later brood, was born, but despite the differences in their ages, all seven of C.Q.'s progeny have enjoyed an enviable family closeness and developed an immense respect for each other. They have been, in athletic vernacular, each other's most enthusiastic cheerleaders, owing in large measure to a father who epitomized pride in heritage and a mother who emphasized family solidarity as the cornerstones of meaningful lives and careers. Little wonder that the Chandlers are referred to as a family of bankers or, equally appropriate, as a banking family.

7

A FAMILY OF BANKERS:
C.Q.'s LATER CHILDREN

The years separating his earlier and later children were preplexing to an aging C.Q. Chandler II. He was 60 when Charley, his oldest son, began his rise in the banking world at Gage, Oklahoma, and 72 when he finally saw Elizabeth (the last of his earlier children) and her husband comfortably settled in 1936 at the First National Bank in Ottawa. He had reached an age at which most fathers can "rest on their laurels" and enjoy their grandchildren. By then, he certainly was enjoying a raft of grandchildren (Margaret's Grace Elizabeth; Charley's Charles Quarles III and Jerome Lewis; Billy's William, Jr., James Jerome, Alice Catharine, and Alfred Arthur; and Elizabeth's Ann Elizabeth), but he hardly could rest on his laurels. Still at home were his three younger children, only Olive of whom had reached her teens. Their careers had yet to be fashioned.

The hyperactivity of the younger children was almost too much for the septuagenarian, especially since 200 South Clifton always was a mecca "for every kid on the block." Alice often relieved the pressures, particularly when C.Q. was at home, by arranging excursions for the youngsters to the river where they spent long afternoons wading and building dams. She also directed that "Mr. Chandler's room is off limits to everyone," and, in deference to his wishes, always insisted that their children be respectful and prompt at mealtimes. "We walked into the dining room," Olive remembers, "exactly at 6:00 P.M. when the clock chimed. There were no excuses for being late. We always ate at a table covered with a white tablecloth and set with sterling silver—and we watched our manners and dined in virtual silence."[1]

Olive was in awe of her father and, at times, a little fearful of him because he lived by an exacting code. She seldom asserted

C.Q. II and Alice in 1927 with their three children, Olive, George, and Anderson.

*C.Q. II holding his infant
daughter, Olive, in 1919.*

herself, preferring to do what was expected without arguing with her father. She rarely spent much time with him but recalls with great affection that he occasionally took her to the bank on Saturday mornings and allowed her to observe the day's activities. When noontime came, he would give Olive some money and ask her to take his private secretary to eat at Innes Tea Room, "which was the place to go for lunch." It was the type of experience a young person cherishes. There were others.

C.Q. often took the entire family to the Wichita Club for lunch following Sunday church services and allowed the children to order their favorite foods, which for Olive always was a club sandwich. However, the most impressive of her "dates" with her father was the annual Rotary Father-Daughter Banquet at which each daughter was given "a sack full of all kinds of goodies and free coupons." Being with father Chandler at such a festive affair was something she has always appreciated as "one of the really neat things" they did together.

There was a special relationship between Olive and her mother Alice, a closeness which grew stronger as the older children left home. They went shopping together, shared many of the same church activities, and spent much time in the kinds of serious and lighthearted talks which mothers have with their daughters.

The C.Q. Chandler II family, children and grandchildren, at Christmastime in 1933.

Like Margaret and Elizabeth before her, Olive was taught to be ladylike and to appreciate and respect the prerogatives of her brothers and sisters. The Chandler household was a happy place for all of them.[2]

Christmases "were just fantastic"because everyone came home for the holidays, including the grandchildren. There always was a massive tree and a big mound of gifts which excited the youngsters "until they were just bursting" to open them. On Christmas morning, C.J. usually served as Santa Claus, and as he performed his functions, the confusion bordered on bedlam. Then, following a sumptuous lunch served around a dining room table which seated 24 people, father Chandler would retire to his room and leave the noise and activities for others to manage.

Olive began her formal education at College Hill School but spent the winter semester of the third grade in Pasadena, California, where Alice had taken her ailing mother to escape the harsh Kansas winter weather. Between school years, she and her younger brothers, George and Anderson, sometimes were sent to summer camp, spending up to ten weeks and "having $25 each to spend anyway we wanted to." She and George usually "ran out of money" a week or two before they were scheduled to leave and would seek loans from Andy, who showed an early skill in managing his allowances.

When she reached high school age, she was told, as had the other Chandler children before her, that she would have to work during the summertime—either at home or at the bank. She chose the latter, and her father found a position for her in the clearinghouse and provided her transportation each day to and from work. Olive persuaded her parents to send her to Stephens College, a women's finishing school in Columbia, Missouri, where she completed her high school studies in the spring of 1936.[3]

Olive then elected to enroll at the College of Emporia. On her first night at college, she met Junius Robert Clift of Augusta, Kansas, a sophomore business administration major, on a blind date. Fate obviously had a hand in the matter, for Olive remembers that young Bob "had the choice between a banker's daughter and a preacher's daughter, and he chose the banker's daughter for his date." It was love at first sight. They were to marry a year and a half later, and the "spurned" preacher's daughter would remain one of their closest friends.

Some coveted honors came to Olive during her short college career. In January of 1937, she was chosen by Guy Lombardo, a nationally famous orchestra leader, from a group of five nominees as the Queen of the College of Emporia. The following September, the popular campus beauty queen was elected president of Chi Epsilon Sigma, the sophomore women's organization at the college. Despite the honors and other involvements in campus activities, it became obvious that she and Bob had fallen deeply in love and were seriously considering marriage.[4]

Having had a similar experience with Elizabeth, C.Q. and Alice arranged an extensive tour of Europe for Olive in the summer of 1937 in the hope that both she and Bob would cool their ardor and decide to finish college before getting married. Olive thoroughly enjoyed the tour and left nothing undone during her weeks abroad, even forfeiting her claim to the promise of

$1000 which C.Q. had made to each of his children if they would not smoke or drink before their twenty-first birthday. She sampled the wines of the masters in France and Germany, more from youthful curiosity than defiance, and she managed to spend most of the traveling money her father had allowed her on "things for my hope chest."[5]

Thus, C.Q.'s efforts were in vain. Bob and Olive waited but a single semester and were married on January 5, 1938, in the Chandler home at 200 South Clifton. The couple moved to California and enrolled at Whittier College. Olive continued until the summer of 1939, dropping out of school shortly before she gave birth on July 4 to their first child, whom they named Robert Chandler. Bob graduated in 1940, and after considering other options, he and Olive decided to join the family of bankers. Father C.Q. built them "a small bungalow" in Carmen, Oklahoma, and assigned Bob to an assistant cashier's post at the First National Bank in that small western Oklahoma town.[6]

As others had done, Bob began his training in a setting C.Q. felt was appropriate, and he made good progress. The following year, Olive bore a second child, Carolyn, on May 18, 1941, but neither success nor family expansion could offset a growing disenchantment with their life in a city of only 900 people. There was little to do, and a minimum of 60 miles separated them from any cultural activities or medical facilities. Alice watched her daughter's depression mount, and a few weeks after Carolyn was born, she told Olive that they were free to make a change if they wished. It was a difficult decision for a couple so young. The natural expectations others imposed on members of the prestigious banking family, plus the immense pressure Bob and Olive placed on themselves during moments of doubt and quiet introspection, caused them to make the decision several times—and each time with opposite results. Finally, the choice seemed clear to both of them. Bob was not overly happy in the banking business, and they both missed the West Coast. Thus, Bob resigned his position, and the Clifts returned to California where they have made their permanent home.[7]

Bob found employment with Douglas Aircraft just as the military buildup began for World War II. Because his assignment

The J. Robert Clift family in 1982, L to R: front row, Brian Laskey, Amy Clift, Olive Chandler Clift, Charles Clift, Jill Clift; second row, Julie Laskey, Chris Laskey, Carolyn Clift Laskey, J. Robert Clift; back row, David Laskey, Robert Chandler Clift, Robert Laskey.

was classified as essential to the war effort, he at first was given a draft deferment but left his post in 1945 to volunteer for duty in the U.S. Coast Guard, although the conflict ended before he was called to serve. For a time after the war, he worked for a men's clothing store, and in 1950 he accepted an assignment as assistant athletic director and bookstore manager at his alma mater, Whittier College. George Allen, now known for his successes in professional football, then was head coach at Whittier and made Bob's return to the school interesting and challenging. Additionally, Richard Nixon, whom Bob knew in his student years, also provided excitement for the institution after he became Dwight Eisenhower's successful running mate in the 1952 presidential elections.

Clift eventually gave up his role in athletics and thereafter was made general manager of the Whittier College Student Union Bookstore. After their children left home, Olive accepted in 1955 a temporary appointment as Bob's secretary and still is employed in that "temporary" position. They "get along beautifully working together" and have found a professional environment and a personal lifestyle which make them happy. Olive maintains close contacts with the Chandlers in Kansas and exchanges occasional visits with her two younger brothers, George and Anderson, both of whom have become successful bankers in different parts of the state.[8]

Since 1948, George has made his home in Pratt, Kansas, but like the other members of the family of bankers, he "traveled a few roads which led to a lot of different places" before he settled permanently in Pratt, a town some 80 miles due west of the city of his birth. He grew up in the family home on 200 South Clifton and discovered, along with Olive and Andy, all of the secret hiding places and play areas in a large and comfortable house which already had accommodated the creative curiosities and antics of four older but equally fun-loving youngsters.

The later children, George remembers, were permitted greater independence within the Chandler behavioral code than his older brothers and sisters, due to the fact that father C.Q. was advanced in years and that he tended to defer to Alice's judgment in raising the younger brood. In fact, it was generally known that when C.Q. proposed marriage, he told Alice that he would be too old to handle additional children, and that if it was her wish to have them, she would have to assume most of the responsibility for raising them. He lived by that dictum; for example, George, Olive, and young Andy often were seen crawling around the floor and under the pews at church while their father listened intently to the sermon and virtually ignored them—something he never would have done earlier— because he felt it was Alice's job to control their behavior.[9]

She did so with love and verbal directions, seldom if ever having to resort to physical punishment. Her style of discipline was based on a full respect for the Chandler code but with an allowance for greater flexibility in its observance. George often pushed that code to the limit and, in his precocity, found himself confronted with stern lectures about proper behavior and attitudes. For example, George was seven when Margaret's wedding was held in the Chandler home. The ceremony was conducted in front of the fireplace, and special pillows had been placed there

George and Olive Chandler being drawn on a sled behind car driven by their mother Alice in 1924. The Chandler home is shown in background.

for the couple to kneel on as they were exchanging vows. It was a grand opportunity for a creative youngster. He fetched his bow and arrow (the type having a rubber suction tip instead of an arrowhead), and before anyone realized what was happening, he had it drawn and aimed directly at Margaret's back at the most critical point in the ceremony. Fortunately he was discovered before he fired the missle. The wedding continued without interruption, but George was hustled off to his room to await his "court-martial."[10]

Privately, the family found the episode humorous and almost entertaining, but C.Q.'s somber face greeted a penitent George as his mother quietly shamed him for his irresponsible behavior. It was typical Chandler punishment, stern but unemotional, corrective but never harsh. Only once does George remember that either parent ever displayed any irritation toward him and admits that he deserved that uncharacteristic reaction. One morning during the depression, young George came to the breakfast table and found his father quietly eating and obviously deep in thought about the alarming number of recent bank failures.

George, standing at left, is pictured with his sister Olive and brother Anderson.

Normally, C.Q. was "a man of iron self discipline," fully capable of ignoring a sleepy-eyed and grouchy 12 year old.

That morning, however, George was acting "just about as nasty" as he could, griping first about one thing and then another until C.Q. apparently reached the limit of his patience. When George complained that there was insufficient light and rose to flip the lightswitch, his father told him to sit down and eat his breakfast, that there was no need for additional light. George obeyed but sulked and refused to eat. C.Q. finished his breakfast and left the house, whereupon the pouting youngster marched over, switched on the overhead lights, and returned triumphantly to the table to eat. Presently C.Q. reappeared, and with "a strength in his voice" George had never heard before, he told his son without rancor but with unmistakable clarity that the light was "going to stay off," that whether or not he ate his breakfast was up to him, but that he would not tolerate being challenged further on the matter. It was a crushing, sobering lesson which George never forgot.

There were other lessons he would learn. As a former teacher, Alice took delight in helping him with his homework and seeing how rapidly she could get him ahead of the rest of his class. He progressed almost too rapidly, being double promoted twice and reaching East High School well in advance of his age group. Along with Alice's determination to make him book-wise, C.Q. made the effort in the summer of 1936 to help him become world-wise. For six weeks, father and son toured Europe together, traveling by train to see historic sites in Ireland, England, Scotland, Belgium, and France and enjoying transatlantic voyages aboard two of the record-setting steamships of the day, France's *Normandie* and England's *Queen Mary*.[11]

During his years in high school, George either miscalculated or received poor counseling; when the time came for him to graduate in 1937, he was informed that he lacked a fraction of a credit and would be required to return in the fall. Both George and Alice regarded it as a waste of time and prevailed on C.Q. to ask Ottawa University, on whose board he served, to make an exception and admit George as a freshman without the high school diploma he never would receive.

One year at Ottawa and another at the University of Wichita proved unrewarding; he was unhappy as a student in business administration and decided to transfer in the fall of 1939 to California Institute of Technology in Pasadena to study engineering, a decision made difficult by his budding romance with Barbara Ann Slothower. The following spring, still mixed up and not very sure of what he wanted to do professionally, George returned to Kansas, went to work in the family bank in Madison, and "began to court Barbara in earnest." Miss Slothower, daughter of the T.H. Slothowers who owned a chain of movie theaters, was a popular member of the younger set who had attended (as had George) both East High School and the University of Wichita. That relationship, however, soon faced a new and more complicated challenge.

The coming of World War II aroused an earlier love. From the time he was a boy, George was fascinated by airplanes. He spent much of his spare time in the early 1930s "hanging around the airport and getting acquainted with the pilots," and willingly took any assignment they gave him if it resulted in a free plane ride. He scrimped his allowances and traded his services for flying lessons. By 1937, a pilot friend, Dave Peterson, permitted him to solo in an open-cockpit Ryan airplane he operated as a flying service. Thereafter, George's love of flying deepened—and was anything but dormant when the U.S. Army Air Corps announced in 1941 a dramatic increase in its training program.

George was eager to get into the program. During the summer, he began the application process, eventually was accepted in November, and ultimately completed his pilot training in July of 1942 at Phoenix, Arizona. Barbara was there to see him graduate, but there was little time for them to discuss their future, although they would announce their engagement later in November. He received orders, along with 100 others in a graduating class of 400, to report immediately for overseas duty in the South Pacific. A series of temporary assignments took him to Hawaii, New Guinea, and back to Hawaii before he was sent to Guadalcanal and attached to the 347th Combat Squadron, the only unit in the South Pacific which was equipped with P-38s.[12]

A series of local newspaper articles, spanning a period of nine months, told of his heroism and promotions. In all, he flew 100 combat missions, shot down five enemy planes, received two oak leaf clusters, and advanced from second lieutenant to major. In February of 1944, he was rotated from his combat assignment to the pilot training program at Chico, California.[13] Home again, he and Barbara completed their plans to be married, and on Thursday, March 16, 1944, they exchanged vows at the Calvary Methodist Church in Wichita "before a throng of wedding guests." Until the war ended, they maintained a temporary home in Santa Monica.[14]

For a time, George felt he had found his niche. He loved flying, and the war created a "sort of swashbuckling atmosphere" which made service-related aviation especially appealing to him. However, as the war drew to a close and the demand for pilot training declined, he found that he was flying less and less and spending increasing amounts of time in administrative trivia. Any thoughts

George Chandler, an ace fighter pilot in World War II, is shown at the time of his graduation from flight school in 1942. Stationed on Guadalcanal, he flew P-38s.

he harbored about making a career in the Air Corps were crushed when he was assigned a non-flying role as the director of a mess hall which fed 300 airmen daily. He resigned his commission at

*After returning from
combat, Major George
Chandler and his new
wife, Barbara, visited
Yosemite National Park.*

Portland, Oregon, in October of 1945 and returned to Wichita,
much in doubt about what he wanted as a career.

"I was very fortunate," George has said, "to have a very dear
brother [Billy Chandler] who had been almost like a father to
me. He very kindly invited me to come to Lyons and go to work
in his bank [the Chandler National] until I could find something
I wanted to do." In March of 1946, George, Barbara, and their
young son (George Throckmorton, Jr., who had been born on
November 3, 1944) moved to Lyons, and became totally involved
in the community as well as the bank. George "got the full treatment," serving in every possible role from teller to credit clerk
to bookkeeper as he sharpened his skills. Then almost too quickly,
Floyd Ross and his family in nearby Sterling offered to sell their
bank to the Chandler interests. C.J. Chandler successfully negotiated a tender offer, and in the summer of 1946, George relocated in Sterling and assumed the management of the Farmers
State Bank.[15]

That move also was temporary. Around Christmastime in 1947,

the George W. Lemon family in Pratt offered to sell their bank, the First National Bank, to the Chandlers. Charles, Billy, and George met with the Lemons in February and drafted a simple, handwritten contract which outlined the purchase agreement. Billy considered but declined the opportunity to move from Lyons to Pratt, whereupon the opportunity was extended to George. He accepted with enthusiasm and promptly moved his family to the new location. "That was the last of March, 1948," George recalls, "and I set my satchel down there, and I've been there ever since—with no real desire to go any place else."[16]

Thus by preference, George Throckmorton Chandler became a small town banker. "There are a great many rewards," he confesses, "to living in a country town. It is a very pleasant way of life. And small town banking is pretty routine because you are on a first name basis with the whole community. Bankers receive a lot of respect and recognition and are expected to provide much of the leadership in guiding the community toward its objectives. Pratt has been awfully good to me and other members of our family."

Indeed it has. The First National Bank of Pratt frequently has been called "the school for young Chandler bankers." George downplays his own importance in helping his relatives learn the banking business, pointing instead to such outstanding professionals as Lawrence Thrall who worked with them on a daily basis in providing hands-on experience in the essential functions of financial management. The indisputable fact remains that First National personnel, from the president to the assistant cashiers, have educated a procession of younger family members, beginning with Chuck (C.Q. III) Chandler in 1949 and followed in quick succession by Billy Chandler, Jr., Jerome Chandler (Chuck's brother), and Arthur Chandler (Billy's brother). Currently, Chuck's youngest son, Robert Paul, has started up the ladder as a beginning banker in the First National Bank of Pratt under the supportive tutelage of his uncle.[17]

George and Barbara are popular members of the Pratt community, as have been their four children, all of whom were raised in the city. George, Jr., (November 3, 1944) was born in Wichita while his father was in the Air Corps, and David Truman (No-

The George Chandler family in 1957, L to R: George holding Paul T.; George T., Jr.; David T.; Barbara holding Barbara Ann.

vember 4, 1947) also was born in Wichita when the Chandlers lived in Sterling. Two other children, Paul Terry (October 28, 1950) and Barbara Ann (August 5, 1952) arrived after the family moved to Pratt. Only David chose to follow the family tradition of becoming a banker. His decision has been a most gratifying development for George, and it has helped him better understand some of the feelings his father experienced.

"One of the great joys of my father's life," George remembers, "was that his son Charley was so close to him and wanted to share so much of his time in both personal and professional matters. Now, at about the same point in my life, my son David is coming along in the banking business and enjoys being with me in the same sort of relationship that Charley and my father had. My association with David in our bank brings me much satisfaction and happiness, and the sharing we now have is as grown men,

The Flying Chandler Family. One of their many flying vacations was a 20,000-mile trip through South and Central America. Shown with their Piper Aztec are L to R: David, Barbara, Paul, Barbara Ann, George.

not just as father and son."That relationship, plus the deep fondness and respect he has for all of his kinsmen, especially his sisters Elizabeth and Olive and his younger brother Andy, are but an extension of the strong family ties which have characterized the Chandlers through the years.

Where once the clan might have been called the Wichita Chandlers, professional obligations and geography have combined to limit personal contacts between them, for the surviving members of C.Q.'s children are spread from Whittier, California, to Topeka, Kansas. Fortunately, George and Bob Clogston (as well as C.Q. III) are board members for the Fidelity State Bank and Trust Company of Topeka which is owned by brother Andy, and the board meetings afford George and Elizabeth (Clogston) the opportunity to visit, if only briefly, with Andy on a regular basis.

Andy, seated in front of Olive and George, is shown riding in an ostrich cart in Pasadena, California, in 1929.

Anderson Woods (Andy) Chandler, seventh and last of C.Q.'s children, has owned the Fidelity State Bank and Trust Company of Topeka since 1958. The road to Topeka for Andy was every bit as plodding as it had been for the others in achieving their goals. Being the baby in the family and younger at least by five years than the other children at home sometimes left a lonely gap between his social life and theirs, but he was much beloved by all of them. The stories others tell of his childhood are warm and affectionately humorous.[18]

There is a delightful tale about one of the few large pets the Chandler children were permitted to have—"a baby lamb which was obtained during a family trip to Coats, Kansas." It was so young that it had to be fed with a bottle. Andy then was a baby, and when he grew hungry and cried, the lamb "would start bleating until he got his bottle too." As he grew older, Andy was permitted first to raise white mice which he trained to pull small carts around on the floor, and later was allowed to keep rabbits, one of which proved embarrassingly hungry on one Easter morning when it ate Mother Alice's orchid corsage.[19]

When Andy was three years old, he inadvertently locked himself in the second floor bathroom, and try as they could, no one seemed to be able to get the door open, nor seemingly could Andy manipulate the latch. Delayed for what seemed an interminably long time, mother Alice could stand it no longer. She called the fire department to "rescue" the trapped youngster. The firemen arrived, and as they were preparing to extend a ladder to the bathroom window, George rushed up the stairs and yelled to Andy that the fire truck was outside. To everyone's consternation—and the firemen's annoyance—Andy quickly unlocked the door and rushed outside excitedly to see "the big red fire truck!"[20]

Like most youngsters, his curiousity sometimes exceeded prudent judgment. George and Olive once caught a bee, placed it in an old Mason jar, and refused to share with Andy the fun they began to have with the entrapped insect. As they shook the jar, the enraged bee made loud buzzing noises which evoked gleeful giggles from its captors. Andy felt rejected and unnecessarily tortured. Thus, when George and Olive left for school, he ignored their orders "to leave that bee alone," and as soon as they were gone, he shook the jar, took off the lid, and promptly was stung—royally. "Served him right," they now tease when the story is retold, to which he laughingly responds, "I fully agree."[21]

There were far more pleasures than pain in those early years. He had pleasant, involved experiences at College Hill and Robinson Junior High schools and was active in Boy Scouts, ultimately achieving 13 merit badges while advancing to a Star Scout ranking. In 1933 at the age of seven, he spent the first of several summers at camp in Colorado, and in 1935 he joined other Wichita youths on a summer tour of the northwestern states. His experiences at camp were memorable, and were highlighted during various summers by attendence at "Frontier Days" in Cheyenne, Wyoming, and by climbing such mountains as Long's Peak. His last year at camp was 1939, after which George drove to Estes Park to bring him home.[22]

Andy attended East High School, graduating in the spring of

The western America summer tour in 1935. Andy is seated fourth from left; Chuck seventh from left.

1943. Too young at 17 to follow George into service, he elected to enroll for his freshman year at the University of Wichita. He began dating Patricia Hinshaw whom he had known at East High, but their budding romance was "put on hold" at the end of the year when Andy persuaded his father to sign the papers permitting him to volunteer for the Air Force pilot training program. His tenure as a cadet was not the best of experiences. For almost 18 months, he was totally frustrated in his efforts to earn his commission, largely because of a severe cutback in the training of pilots. Then, after a two-months' assignment as a B-17 flight engineer in an air/sea rescue squadron, he was presented in November of 1945 with options of resigning from the cadet program and receiving his discharge, or of applying for a transfer to an aerial gunnery school. He resigned and returned home to work at the First National Bank and await the start of the spring semester at the University of Kansas.[23]

Andy had little doubt about what career he would follow. He set a goal of achieving a degree in business administration at KU

Anderson Woods Chandler as an Army Air Force Cadet during World War II.

in order to be better equipped to become a banker. His earliest formal work in the First National started in the summer of 1941, when his father gave him employment as a messenger for the city collection department. In subsequent summers before he entered the Air Corps, he was given greater responsibilities in the credit division and finally in the clearinghouse department. Thus, he was not a novice when he resumed a temporary, three months' assignment in November of 1945. That brief stay in Wichita also allowed him to resume his courtship of Patricia Hinshaw, daughter of Mr. and Mrs. Charles F. Hinshaw, who was completing her coursework at the University of Wichita.

Two and one half years of solid effort at KU brought Andy numerous honors. He was chosen as a Summerfield Scholar, the most coveted scholarship given at KU to a Kansas high school graduate, and to achieve an unfulfilled dream, he enrolled in advanced Air Force ROTC in order to receive a reserve commission "in case there ever was another war." After spending the summer of 1947 in summer camp in Denver, Colorado, he was named the outstanding ROTC student and was offered a regular Air Force commission upon his graduation. Andy also balanced his college studies with some field work in banking, spending the summer of 1946 in a time proven training institution, The First National Bank of Holly, Colorado.

With graduation approaching in June of 1948, Andy made some important decisions. He opted for a reserve Air Force commission, and set the date for his marriage to Patricia Hinshaw for June 14, 1948, one week after he would receive his bachelor of business administration degree at KU's summer commencement exercises. The call to be a banker was too strong; for him there was no other option. The newlyweds had time for only a brief honeymoon in Mexico before they became a part of a "fruit basket turnover" which sent George to the First National Bank of Pratt and Andy to replace him at the Farmers State Bank of Sterling. It was a fortunate, first assignment for the aspiring banker.[24]

Ten happy years in Sterling followed. Andy and Pat (as she was called) bought a home across the street from the Methodist Church and the public library, which was about a block and a

*Opening celebration, Farmers State Bank of Sterling in 1951. Pictured
L to R: Bill Chandler, Jr.; George Chandler; C.J. Chandler; Anderson
Chandler; Frank Smisor; Jim Pate; Kenneth Braley; Bill Chandler; Bob
Clogston; Chuck Chandler.*

half from the Farmers State Bank. Three of their four daughters
were born during their years in Sterling: Cathleen Diane on April
7, 1950; Cynthia Debra on March 17, 1953; and Corliss Denise
on January 22, 1956. Colette Dee, their last daughter, would be
born on February 27, 1961, after the family moved to Topeka.
"It was a nice life," Andy recalls; "I could walk to work, and when
the children came along, they also were within easy walking distance to the grade school. And the Farmers State was an excellent experience for me. There was little inflation in bank deposits
during that decade, but we managed to increase them from about
$1.4 million to $2 million before the opportunity in Topeka
surfaced."

A combination of events paved the way for the move to Topeka. Andy's professional growth slowly generated within him
the desire to own a bank in a larger city, but the right opportunity
did not occur until the Collingwood family decided in 1957 to

The day the Chandlers sold the Kansas State Bank in 1957. In C.J. Chandler's office, W.W. and C.J. are seated, while W.W., Jr., Chuck, George, Jerome, and Andy stand behind them.

sell the Fidelity State Bank and Trust Company of Topeka. Coinciding with that development was the decision by Jim Wilson, longtime local bank president, to liquidate his holdings in the the Kansas State Bank of Wichita, an institution in which the Chandlers had made sufficient investments since the late 1930s to have a majority interest.[25] The Chandlers, along with Wilson, sold their interest in KSB, an action which occurred almost simultaneous with the purchase of the Topeka bank.

In January of 1958, the Collingwoods sold controlling interest in Fidelity State to the Chandlers. Jerome Chandler, C.J.'s youngest son, took over the bank in Sterling, freeing Andy to move to Topeka to begin an orderly transition in the management of the new bank. J.H. Collingwood continued as president of the bank until his retirement in 1961, and on January 4, 1961, the *Wichita Eagle* announced the election of 34-year-old Anderson Woods Chandler "as the youngest man ever to serve as president of the

Topeka bank." Elected with him as members of the board of directors were George and Billy Chandler, Bob Clogston of Ottawa, and C.Q. Chandler III of Wichita.[26]

The potential of Fidelity State had been accurately assessed. At approximately $7 million in deposits in 1958, Andy regarded the bank "as a sleeper with a bright future in one of the most important cities in the midwest." Now at approximately $50 million in deposits, a part of which must be attibuted to inflation, the bank under Andy's leadership also has expanded in physical plant and services. In 1967, a new building was constructed, and after state laws were changed in 1973 to permit banks to have a maximum of three detached branches, the Fidelity State became the first bank in Kansas to open and operate at four separate locations, thus permitting it to offer extended services to its patrons.

From the time he lived in Sterling, Andy has taken an active role in the Kansas Bankers Association and, like his father before him, has been involved in helping to shape state regulations which govern the industry. In recognition of his efforts, his colleagues honored him at the annual meeting of the KBA on May 21, 1982, by naming him president-elect of the Association for 1983, ironically the year which commemorates the 100th anniversary of his pioneering father's entry into the banking profession at Elk City, Kansas. As significant as that honor is, there have been others in which he takes equal pride. He has been president of the Topeka Clearinghouse Association, president of the Topeka Chamber of Commerce, and has been awarded the Silver Beaver Award for prolonged service to the Boy Scouts of America.

No honor, however, exceeds the pride he has in being a Chandler. He once bought two antique cars, autombiles manufactured between 1917 and 1929 under the brand name "Chandler," because he wanted to own a car which bore the family name. He subsequently sold one of them to Grace Braley Jantz, his sister Margaret's daughter in Cherokee, Oklahoma.

Unquestionably, his own family has become a prototype of what has transpired in the development of Chandler family units in the twentieth century. He, like most of his kinsmen, places great

Andy and daughter Colette in his restored 1926 Chandler dual-cowl phaeton.

emphasis upon heritage, but he, like them, places an even higher priority upon promoting closeness between the individual members of his own family. He has great love for Patricia and their four daughters. In earlier years, they traveled together, even sharing a prolonged, funfilled tour of Europe.

More recently, especially since two of their daughters have married, Andy and Pat annually host a family dinner/reunion in Topeka as a way of encouraging all of the girls and their husbands "to come home again." Even more poignant is the practice of sharing a large vacation home in Colorado, a three bedroom house Andy bought and renovated in 1956 but which he since has deeded to his four daughters. The house is used regularly, approximately six times a year, but only by members of the family and the guests they invite. It serves as a safety valve for those who feel the pressures of professional life—and as a sanctuary where all of them can find self renewal in reciprocal affection and concern.

Thus have C.Q. and his children forged a remarkable imprint of professional influence in a continuum now spanning a full

The A.W. Chandler family, L to R: Larry and Corliss Miller, Anderson, Patricia, Colette, Cynthia, Cathleen and David Stevenson.

century and one which may extend well into the twenty-first century through the lives of his younger children—and indefinitely thereafter through those of his grandchildren who have chosen to follow careers in banking.

8

C.Q. III: A THIRD GENERATION AT THE FIRST

The procession of Chandlers at the First National Bank in Wichita has resulted in a confusion of Charleses in identifying its leadership over the years. CHARLES Quarles (C.Q.) Chandler II purchased and directed the bank from 1900 until his death in 1943. CHARLES Jerome (Charley or C.J.) Chandler, his oldest son, served as president and later chairman of the board from 1944 until his death in 1974. Upon C.J.'s death, CHARLES Quarles (Chuck) Chandler III succeeded his father as chairman of the board after having already assumed the presidency in 1971 when Paul Woods retired. And to compound the matter, CHARLES Quarles (Charlie) Chandler IV now is a vice president at the First, and he has a son, CHARLES Quarles Chandler V, who is called "Chuck." Oftentimes, even family members must do a "double take" when attempting to identify one of them properly to someone else.

There is an added confusion. C.Q.'s later offspring were born at approximately the time that his earlier children were marrying and starting their families. Interestingly, the birthdates of C.Q.'s last two sons, George Throckmorton (February 1, 1921) and Anderson Woods (January 21, 1926), place them in a generation simultaneous with that of the earliest sons born to C.J. and Billy. Indeed, Charles Quarles III, C.J.'s first son, was born on September 1, 1926; and William Woods, Jr., Billy's first, arrived the following year on November 26, 1927. In their youth, the boys played more as brothers than as uncles and nephews, with the result that they often behave as brothers in both personal and professional activities—creating an amusing anomaly which sometimes befuddles friends who tend to forget their true relationship. That anomoly, however, explains the camaraderie

The Chandler men in 1929, showing C.Q. II with his sons and two oldest grandsons.

they have always enjoyed and the respect they have had for each other's careers.[1]

The practice of not allowing members of the same generation to serve in the management of the same financial institution set the stage for the progression of leadership at the First National in Wichita, the bank which C.Q. regarded as the parent Chandler institution. As the oldest of C.Q.'s sons, Charles Jerome entered the profession first and had the earliest opportunity to accept an assignment at the First National. In time, he fell heir not only to the management of the bank but also to the leadership of the family. He played a prominent and supporting role in helping his brothers and brothers-in-law acquire the banks they chose to own and direct, and he took care to encourage his own sons, C.Q. III and Jerome Lewis, to develop their talents to the fullest.

When C.Q. III was born in 1926, it was much too early in C.J.'s career for him to have envisioned that his son one day would succeed him as chief executive officer of the First National Bank, or for that matter, that he himself would assume that role. "Chuck was born," Alice Cromwell Chandler reflects, "while we were running a small bank in Gage, Oklahoma, at a salary which allowed us few luxuries. His father and I had only one goal, and that was to see that he had a normal, happy life. We knew if we could accomplish that aim, the future would take care of itself."

Chuck's early life was one of stability and patient, affectionate development. "The nearest thing I had to a hobby," Alice has said, "was my children. I did everything with them. We played just about every game imaginable. On hot summer afternoons, we would start a game and about eight little boys in the neighborhood would begin to show up. I would put them upstairs in the master bedroom where they would beat on the floor and yell until the neighbors must have thought they were tearing the house down. But it was perfectly harmless noise." A surprising number of those early playmates have remained Chuck's closest friends. They attended school together, shared numerous out-of-school activities, and built such enduring relationships that they hold "reunions" periodically in Wichita when those who have pursued careers elsewhere return to the city to visit relatives.[2]

One influential person in Chuck's early life was Ernie Altick, a teacher at Wichita Country Day School who also operated a crafts school known as the Akita Club. One afternoon each week, Altick picked up a number of elementary students and transported them to the Day School where they were taught "all sorts

Chuck (first on left) is pictured with his brother Jerome and their mother, Alice, in 1933.

of Indian lore and crafts." He also conducted summer tours for boys and girls, directing long bus tours to various parts of the country. Chuck, and his Uncle Andy shared one such excursion, a six weeks' trip through New Mexico, Arizona, California, Nevada, Utah, and Wyoming during which they camped out every night and did much of their own cooking. Youthful impressions still are vivid in Chuck's memory—about the awe-inspiring Grand Canyon, swimming in the Great Salt Lake, sweating in the hot afternoon sun at the rodeo in Cheyenne, and the suffering many of the youngsters endured after becoming infected by poison oak during their visit to the Redwood Forest.[3]

Chuck attended A.A. Hyde Elementary School along with two of his relatives: his youngest uncle, Anderson Woods Chandler, who received special permission from the school board to attend the school; and his cousin Elizabeth, daughter of F.O. Carr who was a longtime vice president of the First National. He and Elizabeth were good friends and often played together at her home on Hammond Drive. Both were bright students and were permitted to complete the third grade in a single semester, an event which Chuck views with mixed feelings because they "became mid-semester students."

His teenage years were spent at Robinson Junior High and East High schools. At Robinson, a course in elementary science and an instructor knowledgeable in electricity caused Chuck to develop an interest in becoming an amateur radio operator and inspired him to consider electrical engineering as a career. Later, a high school physics course reinforced both of those ambitions. He was active in other types of activities. When he was 14, C.Q. III took flying lessons but was denied a license when he failed to pass the required eye test. He also cultivated an interest in rifle marksmanship which he perfected during trips to the family cabin on the Ninnescah River, and he was an active member of the East High swimming team.

Photography and stamp collecting occupied his attention for a time, but no hobby was as engaging over a longer time than was his fascination with automobiles. He bought his first car, a 1932 Plymouth Roadster with a rumble seat, when he was 13 years old—almost a year before he was eligible for a driver's license. The car cost $85 and was in such poor condition that it practically had to be rebuilt. It remained in the garage for months while Chuck "tried to find parts, money, and shade tree mechanics" to help him get it in safe operating condition. Then, when he finally secured a license, his less than enthusiastic father agreed to purchase liability insurance provided Chuck worked and earned all operating and maintenance costs.

"Like most Chandler children," Chuck recalls, "I worked at the bank from the time I was old enough to do so, but when I got into the car driving business, I could see that I wouldn't be able to make enough money to keep a car running." To support his hobby, he found a job in a service station on East Central which paid the princely sum of twenty five cents an hour and free oil

Chuck's first new car, a 1946 Ford.

changes. Two years later, he sold the Plymouth, bought a 1938 Ford sedan on which he "lavished [his] money and elbow grease," and after getting it in "super shape," traded the car for a run down 1938 Ford convertible because he thought it would be fun to own one. Gasoline rationing during World War II occasionally posed a problem for Chuck, but his service station customers occasionally shared their unused coupons with him. He seemed always to have enough gasoline to drive his car to school regularly but little for recreational usage.

The war accelerated his education. At 16 in the spring of 1943, he had completed three years at East High and needed only one credit to graduate. Rather than return to high school that fall, he petitioned the University of Wichita for permission to begin his college work and requested that officials at East High accept one of his college courses (college algebra) as a transfer credit in order to fulfill the requirements for his diploma. "Of course there was a war going on," Chuck surmises, "and everyone was being very generous about everything. So, my requests were approved, and I started to college in the fall." The gesture permitted him to complete three semesters before he was inducted in December of 1944 into the United States Navy.

From the various tests he completed during bootcamp at the Great Lakes Naval Training Center, his skills in marksmanship and swimming earned him a period of "relaxed duty" as a member of a regimental rifle team and as a swimming teacher and lifeguard. Later, he was sent to an aviation radar school in Gulfport, Mississippi, after which he was assigned to the Naval Air Technical Training Center in Corpus Christi, Texas, where he served as a radar instructor for the balance of his tour of duty.

Discharged in July of 1946 at Galveston, Texas, Chuck returned to Wichita and made plans to resume the college work he had begun at the University of Wichita. He was determined to become an engineer and first considered attending Purdue University, but he opted instead for Kansas State University where in September he enrolled as an advanced student in electrical engineering, although he "intended to get a dual degree" in business administration. He also pledged Sigma Alpha Epsilon, as had his father before him, and proceeded to become involved in campus activities. At a sorority function, he met Georgia Jeannette Johnson from Council Grove who was scheduled to graduate in the spring of 1948. They did not begin dating immediately, but he eventually invited her to share with him the traditional SAE dinner and dance on March 9, 1947, at which he would celebrate his initiation into the fraternity.

That first date led to full scale romance and eventually to a discussion of marriage. They decided to be practical, to wait until Chuck finished his degree before setting the date. But, when Georgia graduated in May of 1948, the decision was changed. Chuck found a one room attic apartment near the campus; Georgia accepted employment in the college nursery school; and they were married on August 22, 1948, one semester before Chuck was slated to graduate.

The date of their marriage was not the only decision that was changed. After a few semesters of study in electrical engineering, Chuck realized that he would not be happy in that career field, even though he needed only 12 hours to complete the degree. He switched his program to business administration, com-

Chuck and Georgia on their wedding day, August 22, 1948.

pleted an extra semester in business courses, and graduated *magna cum laude* in February of 1949. He was accepted at Harvard University, for classes beginning in the fall of 1950, to start his studies toward an MBA degree, but his marriage and other interests forced him to decline the opportunity.

Not surprisingly, the "other interests" included a growing realization that a career in banking was the wisest and most logical career track. Evidence that Chuck was considering that possibility derives from the fact that he spent his summers working in his uncles' banks, first in 1947 for George at Sterling and then in 1948 for Billy at Lyons, where he helped them install proof systems for deposits, a procedure not then used by most country banks. "Both of them," Chuck recounts appreciatively, "were nice enough to take me and try to teach me something about banking when I really had 'zip' for experience. I had a great time getting to know both of them better; in fact, my summer with George was the first time he and I really had ever spent much time together."[4]

It was George who came to Chuck's rescue after he graduated. "I was nearly out of school," he remembers, "and I didn't have a job. Nobody had said anything to me about going to work, and finally George, who had left Sterling by that time, called and asked if my father had said anything about my coming to Wichita. When I told him he hadn't, George asked if I would like to come to Pratt and work for him. I accepted, and we rented a small trailer and moved our earthly belongings from Manhattan to Pratt."

Thus, a Chandler tradition was extended. Just as his father had done many times, George assumed the responsibility for the professional preparation of another member of the family, and the First National Bank of Pratt became an important first step for Chuck and Georgia. They rented a house about two blocks from the bank, budgeted his monthly salary of $185 to include a net savings of $4, and began making preparations for the arrival of their first child, Jeannette Colleen who would arrive on August 12, 1950. Because several of the young couples with whom they socialized also had small children, the Chandlers fitted comfortably into their new environment.

Shortly after Jeannette was born, Clayton Peffer stopped by the bank in Pratt and asked Chuck to take a coffee break with him. The invitation seemed routine since Peffer headed the correspondent banking department for the First National Bank in Wichita. However, he stated that F.L. Carson, the FNB's board

A Sunday afternoon in Pratt, Kansas, in 1950. Standing L to R: Bill; Bill, Jr.; Chuck; Andy. Seated: Georgia; David; Barbara; Alice Catharine; Throck; Patricia.

chairman, had instructed him to ask Chuck if he had an interest in joining the correspondent division at a salary of $285 per month. As attractive as the opportunity was, the decision to leave Pratt was difficult to make. Not only had Chuck and Georgia learned to love the town and its people, they also had developed a close relationship with George and Barbara, of a type which Chuck "had never experienced with anybody in [his] life." Even Jack Lemon, wealthy former owner of the First National Bank of Pratt, tried to persuade the young couple to remain in the city, but in the end, the appeal of the new opportunity was too great. Chuck accepted the assignment effective October 1, 1950.

For five years, the young banker served in the correspondent division, traveling throughout the states of Kansas, Oklahoma, Texas, Colorado, and New Mexico to call systematically on the approximately 285 smaller banks which kept accounts with the First National. On the bi-weekly trips he made, he sometimes traveled by train and occasionally by air, but he most often drove, averaging over 60,000 miles per year. He was promoted twice during that period, first to assistant cashier and then to assistant vice president, but his chief function remained that of "bank scout," a type of traveling business representative and marketing specialist who sought new bank customers and commercial accounts in addition to servicing the FNB's numerous correspondent banks.[5] Those five years were sometimes lonely for Georgia, but she managed to cope with the situation reasonably well during Chuck's week-long absences. Her life centered around their daughter Jan and their new son, Charles Quarles IV, who was born on July 1, 1953. Additionally, she received much help and support from Alice, her mother-in-law, who reminded her that "every young couple must make sacrifices when they start out, and Chuck won't be on the road forever." Sooner than any of them expected, her prophecy proved to be correct. F.O. Carr's retirement in 1955, after more than five decades of service to the First National Bank, occasioned a shuffling of assignments and created a vacancy in the loan department. To Georgia's great happiness, the position was offered to Chuck.[6]

Thus in 1955, Charles Quarles Chandler III "stopped traveling and became a loan officer with a desk in the lobby and a place to sit down." Life in the bank was significantly different than life on the road—in more ways than he imagined. Shortly after his return, Joyce Richard Courtwright of Newton casually walked up to Mrs. Helen Kruske's teller cage, held out a small bottle, and presented her with a note which read: "I am desperate. Give me the money. This is nitroglycerin. I will blow up the place."

Courtwright fled with approximately $7500 amid excitement never before experienced by FNB personnel, but the saga ended almost as quickly as it began. The felon was apprehended 15 minutes later in the Orpheum Theater where, ironically, the movie "The Tender Trap" was being shown. All of the money was recovered—and the bottle was found to contain only peroxide. Nevertheless, Chuck must have thought it a strange way to welcome a new loan officer.[7]

His new position was the first of some significant promotions which indicated clearly that he was progressing satisfactorily and that he was earning his place alongside the other members of the bank's hierarchy. Within a three-year span, he was elected first to a vice presidency and then to an executive vice presidency.[8] As the *Wichita Eagle* noted in 1959, Chuck did not hold a "paper title":

> Perhaps the point is that Chandler, son of the bank's board chairman and grandson of its founder, is having to work hard for a living. Working in his father's bank, one might think "he had it made." In his case, "having it made" certainly does not mean sitting in an inner office smoking 50-cent cigars ....
>
> At 32, Chandler is a cheerful, modest and able young man, which certainly is why he is liked and respected at the bank for his own sake. It is also why Wichita should be pleased that "Chuck" is making his future in Wichita, rather than elsewhere.
>
> He may, in a sense, "have it made" in his father's bank; but without a doubt, he will make something of his position, the bank, and Wichita. He might be poorer in Jigsaw, N.M., but Wichita would be too.[9]

Those words of praise, which appeared in a column entitled "Wichita Silhouettes," were written to acknowledge the leadership Chuck had given to the FNB's first major progam of building expansion. Between 1956 and 1958, two stories and 6,000 square feet were planned under Chuck's direct supervision and added to the main structure along Douglas Avenue. The new wing opened on May 26, 1958, with photographed fanfare which showed the young vice president as the first depositor at Lillian Childers' teller cage. Even then, his task had not been completed. Thereafter, he coordinated the work of remodeling the old bank lobby to complement and connect with the newer addition.[10]

Throughout the period of construction, Chuck fulfilled his normal duties as a senior loan officer and developed an impressive note case which included transactions with many of the major businesses in Wichita. He also expanded his knowledge of the other functions in the bank by working closely with his father, and by "studying under a perceptive banker like Paul Woods whose leadership in the areas of consumer credit and data processing was of great benefit to the bank." Throughout the 1960s, Paul

Chuck directed the First National's major building expansion in 1957. He is shown with an artist's rendering of the addition.

and Chuck, with C.J.'s support, worked as a team and broadened First National's individual customer base through an innovative and aggressive marketing program which included, among other things, a rapid expansion in the use of the credit card system.[11]

Both men felt that the aura of strict conservatism had hovered too long over the bank's policies. Electronic banking, cash management, and instant credit were revolutionizing the industry and forcing all banks to become highly competitive in an economy burgeoned by rising consumer demands and expectations. The transition was not easy, for the movement toward a more liberal posture posed tremendous philosophical problems for Chuck's father. Unquestionably, it was a big decision for C.J. to abandon the bank's historic concept of trying to keep people out of debt and change to the more contemporary one of allowing, even sometimes encouraging, customers to maintain a status of

Another major construction project was the massive parking garage, shown here before its completion in 1968.

almost constant indebtedness. Had it not been for the admiration and trust C.J. held for Paul, changes in policy might have come even slower than they did. Had Grandfather C.Q. still been alive, it is doubtful that any changes would have occurred.

Improvements were not immediate. The FNB was not much larger by 1965 than it had been in 1945, but a solid policy base had been set. Chuck was given greater freedom in considering loans to firms and individuals whose requests on similar proposals once would have met with summary rejection. He was especially aggressive in searching out potential customers with new business ideas and, as he remembers, "in developing some of the most innovative loan packages in the history of the bank, an incredible number of which have turned out to be good."

The First National, at Chuck's insistence, adopted a liberal attitude toward the loan support program of the Small Business Administration. High failure rates among new business start-ups make many bankers wary of all but the most carefully leveraged financial plans—even those secured by SBA guarantees because they have a tendency to encourage loans which otherwise would not be made. To Chuck, the challenge of identifying potentially successful businesses more than offsets the losses that will result from those which fail. As a result, the First National has been, and is, one of the leading small business lenders in the United States—and has a good track record, so good in fact that Chuck serves on the Small Business Committee of the American Bankers Association and frequently is called upon to be an ABA spokesman during policy discussions with SBA officials in Washington.[12]

By 1970, the FNB was beginning to gain momentum, and deposits for the fiscal year ending on December 31, 1970, showed an increase of more than $40 million over those listed in the 1965 annual report. Barely six months later, one of the chief architects of the new surge announced his retirement. After 43 years of service to the FNB, President Paul Woods closed his note case, moved to an office on the top floor of the building, and reduced his work load to serving on the bank's board of directors and on its trust committee. His retirement was followed by Chuck's elevation to the presidency. C.J.'s death three years later would result in Chuck's appointment to a combined role as president and chairman of the board.[13]

Marvin Barnes, business writer for the *Wichita Beacon*, highlighted Chuck's transition to the presidency by noting that C.Q. III was "the third generation of Chandlers to serve in a top executive post"for the bank. The new chief executive, he recorded, "predicts many changes in the next few years": the elimination of much of the paper work which now plagues the banking business; the extension of new and better services to customers; and an expansion of electronic banking in standardizing and handling more bank functions. These adaptations were essential, the new president prophesied, if the First National hoped to survive in an increasingly competitive market.[14]

Chandler moved with deliberate speed in meeting the challenges he outlined. In August of 1973, the first completely automatic teller in Kansas was installed at the downtown bank—a Burrough's Remote Teller operated by inserting a Master Charge card and punching in a special code number. It was provided mainly for customer convenience "and not to replace the mature

Chuck received this special recognition in the Wichita Beacon when he became president of the First National in 1971.

judgment of a seasoned bank teller." In October, Chuck announced another expansion of services—the proposed construction of two branch banks which ultimately were officially opened in March of 1975. The detached units, one located at Central and Rock roads and the other at Central and Tyler roads, were designed as permanent neighborhood branches to provide checking and savings account services as well as drive-in and 24-hour automatic teller facilities. Obviously, the First National intended to survive.[15]

It did more than survive. There are many ways of assessing the status of a bank, and it has been said that numbers, properly arranged, can be made to prove almost any point desired. And, given even the fact that inflation has added another complication to making comparisons, the following table nonetheless re-

Charles Quarles Chandler III, as president, standing in doorway to the office whose first occupant was C.Q. II. Portrait on wall is of the first C.Q.: Dr. Charles Quarles Chandler of Rocheport, Missouri.

flects a remarkable growth for the First National since "the third generation Chandler" became chairman of the board in March of 1975:[16]

Year	Deposits	Capital, Surplus, Reserve, Undivided Profits	Earnings	Earnings Per Share
1965	$ 99,697,240	$12,466,652	$1,111,656	$22.23
1970	130,565,055	16,912,914	1,889,744	34.36
1975	216,733,334	23,239,890	2,406,644	40.11
1976	238,286,808	25,269,201	2,840,223	47.34
1977	276,630,835	27,298,425	3,025,224	50.42
1978	307,911,037	29,820,008	3,583,582	55.62
1979	356,910,559	33,385,135	4,765,127	75.80
1980	377,392,106	37,774,982	5,733,847	95.56
1981	386,447,100	42,784,384	6,968,402	*58.07 (2-1)
1982	413,074,877	47,541,175	6,684,061	55.70

Much of the change was the result of the new campaign of aggressive marketing and service extension. Detached centers proved their value many times over, but the presence of the new facilities alone did not account for the financial growth of the First National. Some of it came from "a move back to the basics" of personalized banking. Chandler felt that "a bank can have all the money and all the computers in the world and still be out of business."[17] Without the right people handling the customers and operating the new equipment, growth could not be sustained. With the careful selection in 1975 of vice presidents like D.H. Becker to manage the East bank and Phillip T. Miller (1975-1977) and Darwin D. Roberts (after 1977) to direct the West bank, as well as the announced promotion in 1980 of a number of new vice presidents, Chuck has rounded out a team of seasoned professionals—all of whom realize the importance of personalized customer service.[18]

Important also has been a strong internal organization headed (1975-1982) by Executive Vice President R.L. Darmon and a group of senior vice presidents with proven managerial skills who supervise the bank's major divisions:[19]

DIVISION	SENIOR VICE PRESIDENTS	VICE PRESIDENTS
Commercial Loan:	J.L. Wooldridge	C.Q. Chandler IV
		Marijane Hayden
		John W. Long
		R.J. Mosier
		J.P. Naramore
		James C. Oxley
Correspondent Bank:	J.J. Stanley	Lauren W. Kingry
Personal Loan:	C.H. Manahan	
Bankcard:	Dick Wedan	Robert D. Dutton
Marketing:	John J. Luerding	Ralph W. Hight
		C.A. Whitney, Jr.
Investment:	Dorothy Ray	
Operations:	Jolly H. White	R.A. Bumgardner
		R.D. Duphorne
		Gary E. Proffitt
		H.R. White
		Douglas Winkley
Trust:	W.A. Byerley	Steven C. Woods
	E.A. Duguid	Robert Fay
		Elmer L. Pelton
		T.H. Schupp
		Roger W. Zellers
Auditing:	Jay D. Faust, Auditor	Hai Ba Ngo, Trust Auditor

That group of internal operating officers is complemented by an impressive assemblage of men and women who comprise the bank's board of directors. "We probably have," Chuck has said, "the best board of directors of any corporation in Kansas, a very special group of the most influential, most involved people in the state." Through the years, many prominent Kansans have contributed their time and talents to the policy making council of the First National. Those serving in that important function at year end 1982, were:[20]

DIRECTOR/BUSINESS AFFILIATION

H. Marvin Bastian	Chairman of the Board, Fidelity Investment Co.
Duane J. Buckley	Buckley Industries
C. Robert Buford	President, Zenith Drilling Corporation, Inc.
William D. Bunten	President, FNB
Frank L. Carney	Carney Enterprises
F.L. Carson, Jr.	President, Mulvane (Kansas) State Bank
C.Q. Chandler III	Chairman of the Board and President, FNB
George T. Chandler	President, First National Bank of Pratt
R.L. Darmon	Exec. Vice Pres. & Vice Chairman of the Board, FNB
Charles W. Dieker	Senior Vice Pres. & Treasurer, Beech Aircraft Corp.
W.J. Easton, Jr.	President, Easton Manufacturing Co., Inc.
Martin K. Eby, Jr.	Chairman of the Board & President, Martin K. Eby Construction Co., Inc.
Ralph P. Fiebach	Electric Utility Consultant
Paul J. Foley	Chairman, Foley Tractor Co.
Mrs. Pauline B. Gillespie	Investments
Frank E. Hedrick*	Vice Chairman, Beech Aircraft Corp.
H.W. Hill*	Financial Consultant
Charles G. Koch	Chairman, Koch Industries, Inc.
John D. McEwen*	Chairman, Steffen Dairy Foods Company, Inc.
William G. Plested, Jr.*	Investments
Jack H. Rathbone	Oil Operator and Investments
William I. Robinson	Adams, Jones, Robinson and Malone, Attys.
Paul A. Seymour, Jr.	President, Arrowhead Petroleum, Inc.
Donald C. Slawson	Chairman of the Board & President, Slawson Oil Company
John T. Stewart III	President, Plessey Aero Precision Corp.
Patrick H. Thiessen	Cargill, Inc.
Richard W. Volk	President, Energy Reserves Group
Paul H. Woods	Investments

*Denotes Advisory Director

Interestingly, one of the directors, Mrs. Pauline Gillespie, provides an important link with the historical antecedents of the First National Bank. The FNB, it will be recalled, was the result of a merger in 1919 of the Kansas National Bank and the National Bank of Commerce. At the time, Warren Brown was one of the principal investors in NBC. After the merger, Brown became the second largest stockholder in the First National and served on its board until his death, after which his two daughters, Pauline Brown Gillespie and Dorothea Brown Wofford (now deceased), became directors. Mrs. Gillespie remains a major stockholder and is "a very influential businesswoman in Kansas."

In 1982, after months of studying industry trends and analyzing the bank's ability to meet them, Chandler again felt it was time to alter the future direction of the bank. Change has become intergral to FNB's growth. Indeed, change has become endemic to the industry: customers are requiring new and greater services; traditional distinctions between types of financial institutions are disappearing, resulting in increasing competition among them; and legislation and governmental regulations limit the flexibility of banks in adapting to the pressures attending many of the problems they face, including unstable interest rates and inflation.

To meet the challenges, the Board of Directors on November 18, 1982, presented to FNB stockholders a "Plan of Reorganization" calling for the transfer of the ownership of the First National Bank to the First Bancorp of Kansas, a holding company which had been formed in 1971 for subsidiary purposes by C.Q. Chandler III and Paul Woods. Under the plan, each stockholder was to be offered securities of the holding company in exchange for shares of common stock in the bank. Thus, First Bancorp would be owned "by the same persons who currently own the issued and outstanding shares of Common Stock of the Bank." The announced purpose of the transfer was to allow the holding company "to take advantage of the many benefits available to holding companies which are not available to commercial banks," among them being an increased flexibility in conducting certain "non-banking" activities. After November 18, the business of the FNB would be conducted as a wholly-owned subsidiary of First Bancorp. The plan was approved, and an orderly transition was effected.[21]

As a result of the acquisition of the First National Bank by the

Senior management team of the First National Bank in Wichita in 1983. Shown L to R: Charles Quarles Chandler III, Chairman of the Board; William D. Bunten, President; Robert L. Darmon, Vice Chairman of the Board and Executive Vice President.

First Bancorp and the subsequent reorganization, Chuck has retained the office of the chairman of the board and chief executive officer of both entities, but has named presidents for each of them. The highly respected Robert L. Darmon was appointed as president of the holding company while retaining his position as executive vice president and vice chairman of the board of the FNB. For the presidency of the First National, Chandler reached outside to an experienced banker, William D. Bunten, who was then executive vice president of United Central Bankshares, the holding company of the United Central Bank of Des Moines, Iowa.[22]

In making the announcement of his appointment, Chandler noted that Bunten is a native of Goodland, Kansas, and that he is a graduate of two Kansas institutions, Baker University of Baldwin and the Washburn University Law School, as well as the Wharton School of Finance and Commerce at the University of Pennsylvania. Among other positions he has held, the new FNB president also has been the president the Merchants National Bank of Topeka and the chief executive officer of the United Central Bank of Des Moines. "Bunten is an outstanding individual," the *Wichita Eagle and Beacon* quoted Chuck as saying, "and will help us maintain the traditional policies and posture we have built at the First. His understanding of Kansas banking will be extemely valuable in providing assistance to our many correspondent banks."[23]

With two strong presidents in Darmon and Bunten and a new corporate structure which allows the widest flexibility permitted under existing regulations in serving its customers, Chandler is confident that the second largest bank in Kansas is prepared at least for the foreseeable future. The willingness to adapt to change has become the hallmark of the First National and the First Bancorp, a fact that is deeply satisfying to Charles Quarles Chandler III.

There are other sources of satisfaction for Chuck, chief among which is his family. Chuck always has set aside quality time for his wife and children, even in his early career as a traveling representative for the FNB. "When he returned from a trip," his wife remembers, "no matter how tired his was, he always insisted upon diapering, bathing, and feeding the youngsters. He was devoted to them and loved to be involved in every phase of their lives. This was true even after Bob's birth [October 22, 1959], our third child." Later, when the children were older, he and Georgia planned vacations which provided them exposure to some of western America's most scenic wonders, driving many times in recreational vehicles and camping out in the various parks and camp grounds in New Mexico, Colorado, and Arizona. Still later, when he went east on business, Chuck took each of his three children individually on weeklong trips to Washington, D.C., and

*Chuck with Jan, his first
child, in October of 1952.*

New York where father and daughter (or son) shared special experiences together.[24]

Before they went west in 1969, the last major vacation the family would take together, Chuck and son Charlie bought a wrecked Volkswagen and, using the chassis and motor, built a dune buggy complete with a red plastic fiberglass body—and a canopy sewn by Georgia. The vehicle was towed behind a motor home all the way to Lake Powell in Arizona, and was used to make side visits to "just about every Indian site along the way." It also served as a runabout for trips from campsites to nearby cities, and "it was quite a sight" to see the five Chandlers enjoying "togetherness" by crowding into the small craft.[25]

Doing things together as a family always has been important. Since the late 1950s, a ranch and rustic cabin located between Fall River and Fredonia, purchased originally by Chuck's father, has provided the medium for the Chandlers to share weekends of isolated and quiet relaxation. When the children were teenagers, the family went regularly and often took several young friends to enjoy fishing, hunting, and horse riding. Hunting was an interest Chuck and son Bob cultivated together, and when bird seasons opened, they rarely missed a weekend at the ranch.

The Chandler family in Charlie's dune buggy in 1969. Shown L to R: front seat, Jan, Charlie; back seat, Chuck, Bob, Georgia.

Now that their children have left home, Chuck and Georgia still return as often as they can to the cabin where their family has spent many memory-filled times together.

A part of the Chandlers' closeness has resulted from shared religious experiences. Church participation always has been a family affair, but religion to all of them is more than physical attendance at worship services. It is something which is deeply and personally felt. For example, Chuck and Georgia start each day together with a short reading from a daily devotional or from the scriptures, and when the children return home for a visit, they sometimes join together in what they call a "Hymn Sing," a practice initiated at the ranch by Jan as a young girl when she improvised an outdoor sanctuary of stones and wood and, along with her brothers, led the family in singing their favorite hymns in a private Sunday morning worship. Moreover, both Chuck and Georgia have served as lay leaders in the First Presbyterian Church, he as an ordained deacon and a member of the board of trustees, she as an ordained elder and bible school teacher. Religion has been a source of inspiration and happiness to them— and one of the reasons for the closeness of their family.[26]

Chuck with his Brittany hunting dogs, Lisa and Chan, at the family cabin at Fall River in 1976.

Chuck also enjoys in a wide range of business and civic participation. He is a director of several financial institutions, including the First Bank of Newton, the Fidelity State Bank and Trust of Topeka, the Farmers State Bank of Sterling, the Chandler Bank of Lyons, as well as Coronado, Inc., and Lyons Bankshares, Inc. He currently serves also as a director of both the Kansas Gas & Electric Company and the Wichita Club, and is a past president, treasurer, and director of the Wichita Rotary Club. The list of his involvements, past and present, is much longer. C.Q. III has been active in health related organizations such as the St. Francis Hospital Lay Advisory Board (past president and board member), the Wesley Medical Endowment Foundation

Bob, Chuck's younger son, leading morning devotional at the family cabin in 1969.

(chairman and director), and Health Frontiers, Incorporated (director). Other civic endeavors include the Wichita Chamber of Commerce (past director), the Quivira Council of Boy Scouts (past member of the executive board and past treasurer), the Music Theatre of Wichita (director), and the Metropolitan Wichita Council (director and past president). Finally, he has been honored by appointments to the board of trustees for Friends University, the Kansas State University Foundation, and the Wichita State University Endowment Association.[27]

His recent election as president of the Kansas Society for Crippled Children mirrors yet another source of deep pride and happiness. Since its founding in 1925 as a volunatry non-profit organization, the Society has been a Chandler family project, and most members of the clan at one time or another have served on the board of directors or as chairman of one of the 14 districts throughout the state. An impressive number of talented individuals has served the Society with no thought of being compensated by anything other than the satisfaction they derive from working for an organization with such worthwhile goals. Chuck's admiration for those individuals swells whenever he mentions the fact that the Society operates on "just about the lowest overhead of any charitable institution that ever existed because everyone is a volunteer."

The Society complements the Kansas Crippled Children Commission, an agency which was established after the enactment of the Kansas Crippled Children's Law in 1931. The Society is housed in the First National Bank Building in Wichita, and its work is coordinated in such a way that the Society underwrites the costs of the medical or therapeutic needs of physically handicapped children not otherwise covered by state funds under existing laws. "The good that has been done," Chuck reflects, "since my Grandfather founded the Society, has been tremendous. My father also found the work very rewarding, as have all the rest of us because we have seen so many young people receive the help they needed to become productive citizens in our state."[28]

There is another involvement which links Chuck to an activity his father initiated and enjoyed—the monthly "silent meditation" services for businessmen. After C.J. died in 1975, Floyd Amsden took the lead in sending reminders and making arrangements for the sessions at the First Presbyterian Church. Chuck continued as a participant until Amsden passed away in 1980, after which he assumed the role of mailing notices of the meetings to some 50 individuals. A few of them no longer live in Wichita and are unable to attend, but they insist upon being kept on the mailing list because they enjoy receiving and reading the announcements which contain selected inspirational messages, all of which were originally compiled or written by Charles Jerome Chandler and which since have been reused by both Amsden and Chuck.[29]

Chandler believes he has been singularly blessed by such experiences. He also takes much pride in the success and happiness which his brother Jerome, with whom he remains close, has enjoyed during his residence in Sterling and his work at the Farmers State Bank. And, happiness of a type which only a Chandler father can understand has come from the fact that Chuck's two sons have chosen to extend the family's unique legend by becoming bankers, Charlie at the First National in Wichita, and Robert Paul at a time-proven educational institution, his great-uncle George's bank in Pratt. Thus, the future portends an expanded prologue for subsequent members of a banking family.

9

THE CHANDLERS OF KANSAS: AN EPILOGUE

A feature story in March of 1975, published in the *Wichita Eagle and Beacon*, paid the Chandlers of Kansas an eloquent compliment. "Mention the name Chandler in business circles around Kansas," the article began, "and a good many persons would spell the name B-A-N-K. And for good reason. The late C.Q. Chandler, founder of the First National Bank in Wichita, persuaded a good many of his progeny to enter the business, and Chandler bankers now proliferate throughout the state."[1]

All of C.Q.'s sons (C.J., Billy, George, and Andy), the *Eagle and Beacon* reported, are or have been bank presidents; three of their sons (Billy, Jr.; and C.J.'s two sons, Chuck and Jerome) already have achieved that high position; and James (Billy's second son) then was serving as vice president and cashier of the First National Bank of Ottawa. The account was quite impressive but could have been even more so had C.Q.'s sons-in law (Kenneth Braley and Robert Clogston) been included within the family's roster of bank presidents.

The article, written in recognition of Chuck's election as FNB's board chairman, gave some well deserved visibility to another Chandler who has made positive contributions to the family legend. By 1975, Jerome Lewis Chandler, C.J.'s youngest son, already had served for 17 years as president of the Farmers State Bank in Sterling, having replaced Andy in 1958 when he moved to Topeka.

During his tenure as its chief executive officer, Jerome has built the FSB from a small institution to what is now the leading bank in the region. The Farmers State has substantial influence in Rice County, owing principally to his outstanding talents in public relations and in knowing what it takes to develop a large com-

Christmas in 1954 at the Jerome Chandler home in Pratt, Kansas. Pictured L to R: Jerome, Lois, Alice with Kim, Charley with Jan, Chuck, Georgia with C.Q. IV.

munity bank. Because of his achievements, Chandler has been recognized professionally by state and national banking organizations and for years has been one of the leaders in the Kansas Bankers Association and the American Bankers Association.

Jerome grew up in the same household with Chuck, and although born four years apart, their early patterns of development were remarkably similar. Educated in the Wichita public schools, Jerome was an outstanding student who left little doubt in anyone's mind about what career he would follow. When he was 14, he asked his father to find employment for him in a bank, and through James Wilson at the Kansas State Bank, Charley arranged for him to work at various jobs each summer at KSB until he graduated in 1948 from East High School. He then made plans to join Chuck at Kansas State University, but went temporarily to Cherokee, Oklahoma, where he gained additional experience in his Uncle Kenneth Braley's bank until the fall semester began. Thereafter, his years of study toward a degree in economics at KSU were interspersed with summer assignments at the First National Bank in Wichita. Only a stint in the U.S. Air Force (1952-54) during the Korean War delayed the formal beginning of his career in banking.[2]

During his freshman year at Kansas State, he met Lois Gillan from Concordia, also a freshman, and a relationship of deep affection grew until they made permanent commitments to each other, although both fully expected to receive their degrees before they were married. However, Jerome had enrolled in advanced ROTC a few months before the Korean conflict began, and because he anticipated a call to service upon his graduation, he and Lois persuaded their parents to allow them to marry during the spring of 1951 so that they could enjoy a year together before he received his military assignment. They both graduated in the spring of 1952, and Jerome was named the distinguished military student. He was offered a permanent Air Force commission, but he decline the opportunity because he wanted a career in banking, not the military.

Two years of service followed, most of which he spent as a finance officer at Warner Robbins Air Force Base near Macon, Georgia. His duty assignments were enjoyable, and Lois worked at the First National Bank of Macon until Karen Alice (Kim), their first child, was born on December 19, 1953, a little more than six months before Jerome's enlistment expired. After his discharge in August of 1954, Jerome was eager to accept a permanent banking appointment. As much as he would have enjoyed returning to Wichita, he knew the Chandler rule only too well. Chuck already was employed at the First National in Wichita; thus, he would be obliged to begin elsewhere. Again, Uncle George supplied the opportunity, as he had for others in the past, and Jerome and Lois moved to Pratt.

"We went to Pratt," Jerome has said, "with the sole idea of staying there for the rest of our lives. Had it worked out that way, neither of us would have been disappointed, because our experiences in Pratt were unbelievably rich and rewarding. I learned the most valuable banking lessons of my life, and Lois and I had a very happy home and community life." They were destined,

Jerome and Lois Gillan were married on May 27, 1951.

however, to remain in Pratt for only four years. A few months after Charles Jerome II, their second child, was born on May 25, 1957, the opportunity Jerome had dreamed of (but dared not

Charles Jerome Chandler with his namesake, grandson Charles Jerome II, born May 25, 1957, in Pratt.

anticipate) became available when Andy acquired the Fidelity State in Topeka and offered the bank in Sterling to Jerome. It was an offer he could not reject.

In March of 1958, Jerome moved Lois and their family to Sterling and assumed the presidency of the Farmers State Bank. Sterling has been everything they had hoped it would be. He and Lois have been exceptionally happy and have never considered leaving. Both of their children grew up in the town, had excellent school experiences there, and later graduated from Kansas State University. And, after the children left home to pursue careers of their own, Lois went to work alongside her husband at the Farmers State Bank.

Jerome's personal life has been one of contentment. He enjoyed an unusually warm relationship with his father, often exchanging handwritten letters with him in which pithy "quotes-of-the-week" and moral messages were shared. One of his most cherished keepsakes is a small, multilithed booklet of humorous banking tales, entitled "Nine Percent Interest and Other Stories," which C.J. compiled and mailed to his closest friends. Another close relationship he shares is with his brother Chuck, both of whom regard their ability to communicate openly and freely as one of life's rarest blessings.

And, Jerome's professional life has been one of achievement. A vital part of that life is his devotion and unselfish commitment to the city's various civic and business activities, including the numerous programs sponsored by the Chamber of Commerce and Rotary International. Sterling College, a small Presbyterian school which is "the pride of Sterling," owes a genuine debt to Jerome for his patient counsel and persistent work in promoting the school's financial stability. He first was elected to the board in 1961, and the following year was named chairman of the institution's Board of Trustees, a position he has held without interruption since that time. He has been a stalwart in raising scholarship funds for students who wish to attend Sterling College and is the school's representative to the Association of Colleges in Central Kansas, a foundation for private colleges in the state.

His involvements external to Sterling are numerous. Like most Chandlers, he takes an active interest in and serves as a director of the Kansas Crippled Children's Society. He has had a long involvement with the National Junior College Athletic Association and currently serves as its financial adviser. But, perhaps the oldest and most cherished of his personal commitments has been to Kansas State University, his alma mater. An avid "Wildcat," he enjoys a spectator's enthusiasm for the KSU sports program, and devotes considerable time each year to the university as a member of the board of the Endowment Association, as a trustee of the Alumni Association, and as a regional chairman for the President's Club.

In addition to being active in the Kansas Bankers Association, he also serves as a director of the Kansas Bankers Surety Company. And significantly, Jerome has gained more visibility than any previous Chandler in the American Bankers Association, having served as head of its Community Bankers Division for several years. He is called upon frequently to represent the Association as a speaker on the national level, and has taught classes

Jerome, who was awarded an honorary doctorate from Sterling College, welcomes football star Roosevelt Greer to a special event at the College in 1982.

at such universities as Rutgers, Nebraska, and Kansas State. As a member of the third generation of Kansas Chandlers, Jerome has done his part in perpetuating the family legend, as have both of his children who have followed careers in the financial world, though they are not now Kansans.

Perhaps the test of endurance for the Chandler banking legend in Kansas now lies more directly on the shoulders of a fourth

The Jerome Chandler family, L to R: standing, Jerome, Charles Jerome; seated, Lois, Kim.

generation, members of which are just beginning to find their places in the natural order of leadership progression. David Truman Chandler, George's son, has begun his rise alongside his father in the First National Bank of Pratt, an association which is exceptionally pleasing to George and one which portends uninterrupted Chandler leadership for the Pratt bank. The youngest member of the fourth generation is Robert Paul Chandler, Chuck's younger son, who accepted in 1982 his first bank ap-

Sigma Alpha Epsilon is a family tradition dating to C.J.'s days at Centre College. Shown at Bob's initiation at Kansas State University in 1979 are fraternity brothers, L to R: Jerome, Charlie, Chuck, Bob, and (brother-in-law) Steve Randle.

pointment at the First National in Pratt following his graduation from Kansas State.[3]

Chuck's oldest son, Charlie, is the fourth Chandler to wear the name Charles Quarles and fourth to serve as an officer of the First National Bank in Wichita. Like his father before him, he entered Kansas State University with mixed feelings about a career in banking, and chose at first to pursue a program in pre-law. But, he had been exposed at an early age, as have most Chandler children, to his family's profession, and by the time his freshman year at KSU drew to a close, he realized that he could no more avoid the inevitable than his father did. He switched majors and ultimately graduated *cum laude* with a degree in finance during the 1975 KSU spring commencement exercises.[4]

He had met Marla Zarda while they were students together at

*An honor student at
Northwestern University,
Charlie is shown with his
father, Chuck, on
graduation day in 1976.*

KSU and their relationship had become serious, but Charlie was
not yet satisfied with his professional preparation. He postponed
all marriage and career plans and made application at Northwestern University to study for a Master of Management degree.
In completing that application, one of the questions asked him
to state his reasons for wanting to enter the program. According
to his mother who typed the forms for him, his answer was: "If
I go to work for the First National Bank in Wichita, I will be the
fourth Charles Chandler to be connected with that institution.
I will need all the education I can get to prove myself as an
individual."

He was accepted and enrolled in the fall of 1975. A year of
intensive research and study, much of it in the area of electronic
fund transfer systems, earned him recognition as a distinguished scholar upon his graduation of 1976. His attention then
was redirected toward the delayed aspects of his life—personal
and professional—both of which had been carefully planned.

On July 17, 1976, he married Marla Zarda, herself a graduate
of Kansas State University and the daughter of the Bernard Zar-
das of Kansas City, Missouri. After spending their honeymoon
in southern California where they visited leisurely with Bob and
Olive Chandler Clift, the couple returned to Wichita to assume

The wedding of Charlie and Marla on July 17, 1976, was a family affair.
Shown L to R: Steve Randle holding Ariella, Jan, Marla, Charlie, Geor-
gia, Chuck, Bob.

the staff position at the First National which Charlie had been
offered. For two years, he was assigned to special projects, one
of which was in the area of his graduate studies—the development of an electronic fund transfer system for the FNB. Grad-
ually, he became involved in making commercial loans, and after
1978 was assigned almost exclusively to that area. In the short
period of three years, he built a substantial loan portfolio and
was promoted first to assistant vice president and later to vice
president in the Commercial Loan Division which is headed by
Senior Vice President J.L. Wooldridge.

The Chandler mystique surfaces periodically when others appraise the solid progress Charlie has made in a few short years.
"Everyone in the banking community," a close friend of the family once remarked, "knows that there always has been a Chandler
at the helm of the First National, and knows also that if the tradition is to continue, Charlie is the logical person to do it. But,

Charlie joined his father at the First National upon his graduation and has enjoyed a rapid growth in responsibilities.

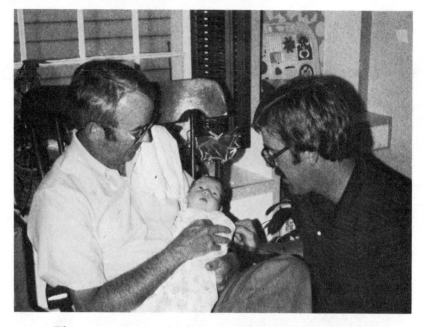

Three generations—Charles Quarles Chandler III, IV, and V.

you can be absolutely sure of one thing; it won't be handed to him. He"ll have to earn it."[5]

Earning one's way is well established as a Chandler tradition, but deciding what goals are to be achieved always has been a private matter for the individual determination of each family member. For example, Jerome Chandler could find fulfillment in Sterling while his brother Chuck was finding his challenge in nearby Wichita. Whatever motivates Charlie in setting personal and professional goals is something he holds quietly and personally to himself. His priorities, however, become visible by observing his activities.

It is obvious that his family is important to him. On a recent "Goodwill/Trade Mission" to London, sponsored by the Wichita Area Chamber of Commerce on whose board of directors he serves, he spent much of his unscheduled time in relaxed, private sightseeing with Marla and in purchasing gifts for their young son, Charles Quarles Chandler V, who was born on August 14, 1981.[6] The Wichita Chamber is but one of numerous civic activities in which he is involved. He is a Rotarian, and holds responsible positions in Big Brothers-Big Sisters (vice president), United Way (director), Kansas Society for Crippled Children (treasurer), Institute of Logopoedics (trustee), and the Sedgwick County Zoological Foundation (treasurer). He also is an active member of the Eastminister Presbyterian Church and the Downtown Y's Men Club. Time, commitment, and ability ultimately will converge with appropriate opportunities and help him reach the unexpressed, and perhaps not yet fully developed, goals and ambitions he has set for himself.

Another unmistakable observation is the obvious admiration he and his father have for each other. They share many avocational interests, such as ham radio operations, and they are avid supporters of Kansas State University athletics, oftentimes starting after work and driving round trip between Wichita and Manhattan to attend Wildcat basketball games.[7]

They also share similar professional philosophies and recognize not only that future challenges for banks like the First National will continue to be intense but also that some excellent opportunities will emerge for those who are prepared to take advantage of them. Perhaps it is for that reason that Chuck recently appointed a type of "blue sky," brain-storming committee, composed of some of the bank's younger executives, and charged it with the task of "dreaming on the wild side" of emerging issues and developments which might affect the FNB. Significantly, Charlie was named to chair the committee.

As important as it is to peer into the future, it is equally important not to neglect earlier moorings. As one of C.J.'s favorite quotes-of-the-week reads, "A man who denies his heritage, has none." For the Chandler family, maintaining a respect for family and heritage always has been a matter of the highest priority, and each generation has furnished at least one person whose responsibility it is to do whatever seems appropriate to cultivate a pride in family achievements, and to encourage closer cooperation and contact between the various family members. Each of them has approached the responsibility differently but has enjoyed equal effectiveness in achieving desired objectives.

Grandfather C.Q. compiled an elaborate documentary on the

Chandlers in America and by example taught his children to revere their ancestry. C.J. was less of a researcher, but he made excellent contributions to the solidarity of the family through his affectionate leadership and unselfish handling of the family trust. George became the leader after C.J. died. However, as early as 1964, he made a pilgrimmage to Virginia in order to visit the colonial estates of the Chandler ancestors, and he was so inspired by the experience that he became the family genealogist. His first detailed compilation was produced in 1966, but it has been twice updated, once in 1978 and again in 1982.[8]

In more recent times, Chuck has shown an increasing sensitivity toward ancestry and heritage, largely because he fears that the younger generation of Chandlers (and those yet unborn) will grow up without knowing much about the history and accomplishments of their forebears. Perhaps, too, Chuck has become motivated because he finds that he has little knowledge himself about the earlier Chandlers, despite the fact that all of the materials which his grandfather collected and compiled in numerous scrapbooks are now housed in credenzas and cabinets in his (Chuck's) office in the First National Bank. Having that data synthesized and developed into a usable family history has become his goal.

June 13, 1983, is a significant date in the history of the Kansas Chandlers because it marks the 100th anniversary of Grandfather C.Q.'s formal entry into the banking profession in Elk City, Kansas—a full century during which one man and his clan have made the profession a family affair. A special observance will be held to commemorate that important beginning and to remind Chandlers young and old that their inheritance truly has been unique. That celebration, however, will be but the continuation of a conscious effort which has been ongoing for many years to build stronger relationships between the various members of the family.

That effort began shortly after World War II when C.Q.'s seven children jointly purchased a small ranch in the historic Flint Hills of Kansas. C.J. Chandler initiated the idea, and he found willing partners after he, Billy, and Andy located, and arranged to buy from the John Drummond Estate, 982 acres of unspoiled grassland in Chase County, "with the understanding that each of the seven had an undivided one-seventh interest in the property."[9]

The acquisition was made more as a unifying gesture than as an investment, and it has been used extensively by family members for recreational purposes. Various improvements have been made through the years to render it more attractive as a type of rustic resort and picnic center in a "back to nature" format. Few permanent structures have been erected other than restrooms and a watershed dam which impounds sufficient water for fishing and boating. Also, a small recreational area has been fenced and developed into a park which contains only a picnic shed with tables. It has become known unofficially as the C.J. Chandler Memorial Park.

Every summer for the past several years, a picnic retreat has been held for all male family members who are ten years or older. Its purpose is two fold: to encourage closer relationships by increasing their knowledge of each other's interests and accomplishments, and to span the generations by involving men of all ages in common activities. Despite the good-natured "scorn" the womenfolk cast upon this annual outing, the results have been gratifying. The younger boys eagerly await the year they can qualify for membership, and the older men happily anticipate the opportunity to share a few fun-filled days with those to whom the future must be entrusted.

It is the Chandler way of building pride in a common heritage and of instilling respect for individual interests and achievements. But, there even is a deeper significance. Perhaps a prominent educator once worded it best in this succinct, prophetic statement: "We need often to return to the bosom of our families, for it is only in their hearts that we truly live and, just as surely, by their loving hands that we shall be buried."[10]

The 1982 annual picnic at Hymer, the family ranch in the historic Flint Hills, showing the male members (ages ranging from 14 to 75) of the Chandler clan in attendance.

Appendix
THE KANSAS CHANDLERS
1864-1983

The genealogy which follows has been adapted from George Throckmorton Chandler's, *The Chandler Family, 1637-1982*, a copy of which is in the *Chandler Collection*. In order to remain consistent with the title of this book, only direct descendants of C.Q. Chandler II have been included hereafter; however, the pre-Kansas Chandlers, beginning with 1577, are treated in Chapter 1.

For convenience, a simple format has been employed: (a) Generation #1, an identification of C.Q. Chandler II's children; and (b), Generation #2, a listing of each of his children (shown in capital letters) and the developments (in numbered sequence denoting subsequent generations) of their respective families.

GENERATION #1	Birth	Death
Charles Quarles Chandler II	Aug 18, 1864	Dec 19, 1943

Married Lizzie Hall Wright (Oct 10, 1887)
Deceased (July 4, 1889), no children.

Married Olive Frances Thayer (June 22, 1898)
Deceased (Aug 2, 1915), four children:

2A Margaret Chandler	Sep 8, 1901	Apr 22, 1955
2B Charles Jerome Chandler	Nov 15, 1902	Dec 15, 1974
2C William Woods Chandler	Mar 17, 1904	Jan 5, 1979
2D Elizabeth Chandler	May 26, 1906	

Married Laura Alice Throckmorton (Sep 5, 1917)
Deceased (Jan 20, 1969), three children:

2E Olive Frances Chandler	Jan 25, 1919
2F George Throckmorton Chandler	Feb 1, 1921
2G Anderson Woods Chandler	Jan 21, 1926

GENERATION #2

2A MARGARET CHANDLER

Married Kenneth Gerald Braley
(Apr 25, 1935), one child:

3A Grace Elizabeth Braley   Nov 26, 1936
Married Roy Janz
(May 6, 1960), one child:

     4A Michael Roy Janz   Dec 29, 1963
     Married Beverly Ann Ivy
     (June 25, 1982), no children.

2B CHARLES JEROME CHANDLER
Married Alice Ewing Cromwell
(Apr 12, 1925), two Children:

3B-1 Charles Quarles Chandler   Sep 1, 1926
     III
     Married Georgia Jeannette Johnson
     (Aug 22, 1948), three children:

     4B-1 Jeannette Colleen   Aug 12, 1950
       Chandler
       Married Steven F. Randle
       (Dec 27, 1970), two children:

       5B-1 Ariella Jeannette Nov 19, 1973
         Randle
       5B-2 Schehera   Jan 26, 1978
         Fielding Randle

     4B-2 Charles Quarles   July 1, 1953
       Chandler IV
       Married Marla Jean Zarda
       (July 17, 1976), one child:

       5B-3 Charles Quarles Aug 14, 1981
         Chandler V

     4B-3 Robert Paul Chandler Oct 22, 1959

3B-2 Jerome Lewis Chandler   Sep 16, 1930
     Married Lois Gillan
     (May 27, 1951), two children:

     4B-4 Karen Alice Chandler Dec 19, 1953

4B-5 Charles Jerome   May 25, 1957
    Chandler
    Married Elizabeth Lester Hund
    (Dec 29, 1979), no children.

2C WILLIAM WOODS CHANDLER

Married Thelma Gillespie
(Aug 28, 1926), four children:

3C-1 William Woods Chandler, Jr. Nov 26, 1927   Aug 2, 1979
    Married Geneva Cordell (Oct 11, 1960)
    Divorced (Dec 3, 1976), no children.

    Married Mary Elizabeth Smith
    (Dec 23, 1977), no children.

3C-2 James Jerome Chandler   Aug 3, 1929
    Married Judith Rombold (Sep 6, 1952)
    Divorced (Oct 21, 1977), three children:

    4C-1 Christine Wahleehah   Feb 15, 1956
        Chandler
    4C-2 Mary Thelma   Apr 21, 1959
        Chandler
    4C-3 James William   Aug 5, 1961
        Chandler

    Married Gwendola Ann Pederson
    (Mar 4, 1978), no children.

3C-3 Alice Catharine Chandler   Feb 1, 1931
    Married Frank Carmine Sabatini
    (Dec 28, 1954), four children:

    4C-4 Frank Marcus Sabatini Sep 23, 1955

    4C-5 Matthew Carmine   Jul 14, 1957
        Sabatini
        Married Trudy Lynn Perkins
        (July 5, 1980), no children.

    4C-6 Michael William   Sep 27, 1959
        Sabatini
        Married Cynthia Lucille Bernica
        (May 23, 1981), no children.

4C-7 Daniel Martin Sabatini Dec 26, 1961

3C-4 Alfred Arthur Chandler   Feb 15, 1932
Married Patricia Ann Reynolds (Nov 5, 1954)
Divorced (Mar 2, 1971), five children:

4C-8 William Woods   Jun 13, 1955
Chandler III

4C-9 Deanna Carol   Mar 31, 1957
Chandler
Married Brian Frisco (May 17, 1975)
Divorced (July 10, 1981), one child:

5C-1 Brooke Rene   Oct 8, 1980
Chandler

Married James Lee Swalley
(Sep 17, 1981), no children.

4C-10 Gretchen Patricia   Jan 11, 1959
Chandler

4C-11 Sara Rene Chandler Jan 11, 1959
Married Floyd James Swalley
(June 6, 1981), no children.

4C-12 Andrea Susan   Dec 30, 1961
Chandler

Married Mary Margaret Ives Farley (Mar 8, 1971)
Divorced (July 5, 1979), no children.

Married Crysta Jean Coxon Christmann
(Mar 17, 1981), no children.

2D ELIZABETH CHANDLER

Married Robert M. Clogston
(Oct 27, 1928), one child:

3D Ann Elizabeth Clogston   Oct 24, 1936
Married Trexel Warren (Nov 28, 1954)
Divorced (Sept 27, 1961), three children:

4D-1 Stephen Robert Warren Oct 20, 1956
Married Donna Marie Swallow (Dec 17, 1977)
Divorced (Aug 2, 1978), no children.

4D-2 Lisa Anne Warren   Apr 7, 1958
Married Wes Owen Brant
(May 27, 1978), one child:

    5D-1 Michael Cole   Sep 17, 1982
    Brant

4D-3 Sara Lynne Warren   Oct 25, 1960

2E OLIVE FRANCES CHANDLER

Married J. Robert Clift
(Jan 5, 1938), two children:

3E-1 Robert Chandler Clift   July 4, 1939
Married Judith Adele Whiteman (June 16, 1961)
Divorced (1971), three children:

    4E-1 Amy Alice Clift   Dec 25, 1961
    4E-2 Jill Ellen Clift   May 24, 1963
    4E-3 Walter Charles Clift   Apr 22, 1966

Married Dorothy Ann Green (Oct 17, 1971)
Divorced (1977), no children:

3E-2 Carolyn Clift   May 18, 1941
Married Robert Edward Laskey
(Sep 11, 1959), five children:

    4E-4 Christine Ann Laskey   Mar 22, 1961
    4E-5 Michael Edward Laskey Jun 11, 1963   Sep 1, 1963
    4E-6 Julie Susan Laskey   May 28, 1964
    4E-7 David Edward Laskey   Mar 27, 1965
    4E-8 Brian Robert Laskey   Dec 27, 1971

2F GEORGE THROCKMORTON CHANDLER

Married Barbara Slothower
(Mar 16, 1944), four children:

3F-1 George Throckmorton   Nov 3, 1944
Chandler, Jr.
Married Janie Kathleen Stewart (Feb 14, 1964)
Divorced (Feb 1970), three children:

    4F-1 Charles Paul Chandler Sep 18, 1965
    4F-2 George Throckmorton May 29, 1967
    Chandler III

4F-3 Richard Anthony   July 3, 1968
    Chandler

Married Virginia Lee Lofdahl
(Sep 26, 1970), two children:

4F-4 Ty Lynn Chandler   Nov 21, 1962
    (adopted)
4F-5 Thomas Wayne   Sep 9, 1963
    Chandler (adopted)

3F-2 David Truman Chandler   Nov 4, 1947
Married Michele Harmon
(Oct 24, 1969), two children:

4F-6 Robert David Chandler June 3, 1970
4F-7 Brian Scott Chandler   May 13, 1977

3F-3 Paul Terry Chandler   Oct 28, 1950
Married Nilda Madrid
(Jan 3, 1977), no children.

3F-4 Barbara Ann Chandler   Aug 5, 1952
Married Donald Keith Jordan
(Sep 6, 1975), one child.

4F-8 Travis Chandler Jordan   Jan 21, 1983

2G ANDERSON WOODS CHANDLER

Married Patricia Hinshaw
(June 14, 1948), four children:

3G-1 Cathleen Diane Chandler   Apr 7, 1950
Married David Alexander Stevenson
(Aug 13, 1977), two children:

4G-1 David Alexander   Oct 22, 1980
    Stevenson, Jr.
4G-2 Lauren Cathleen   Sep 9, 1982
    Stevenson

3G-2 Cynthia Debra Chandler   Mar 17, 1953

3G-3 Corliss Denise Chandler   Jan 22, 1956
Married Larry Collins Miller
(June 9, 1979), no children.

3G-4 Colette Dee Chandler   Feb 27, 1961

NOTES

Chapter 1

[1] Sarah Ann Quarles Chandler, Diary of A Trip From Virginia to Missouri, [September 17 to November 8] 1836. Parts of the diary were serialized in the *Boonville (Missouri) Weekly Advertiser*, January 25; February 1, 8, 25; and March 8, 1935. Copies of the diary and the news articles are in the *Chandler Collection*.

[2] The Lineage of Richard Chandler (1577-1623), typescript in *Chandler Collection*.

[3] "The Name and Family of Chandler," *Genealogy and Historical Sketch* (Washington, D.C.: Media Research Bureau, 1924), pp. 2-3.

[4] [Genealogy of] Charles Quarles Chandler II, typescript in *Chandler Collection*.

[5] The compilation which follows is taken from numerous documents collected over several years by Charles Quarles Chandler II from a number of unidentified sources. The basic facts in each document are duplicative, but each source adds interesting anecdotes to the story of the Chandlers in America. The documents, are entitled: The Lineage of Richard Chandler (1577-1623); The Genealogy of the Chandler Family; The Chandler Family, 1637 to 1966; and, Children Born to Leroy Chandler and His Two Wives, Eloisa Riddick Copeland and Sarah Ann Quarles. All of these studies may be found in the *Chandler Collection*.

[6] *Ibid.* The description of each generation head which follows, unless otherwise specifically documented, is drawn from the one or more of the sources cited above.

[7] Marshall Wingfield, *History of Caroline County, Virginia* (Richmond, Va.: Trevvet Christian and Co., Inc., 1924), p. 401.

[8] Garland Ferrell to C.Q. Chandler II, February 27, 1932; Wingfield, *History of Caroline County*, p. 401.

[9] Genealogy of the Chandler Family, typescript in *Chandler Collection*.

[10] Wingfield, *History of Caroline County*, p. 401.

[11] Malcolm H. Harris, *History of Louisa County, Virginia* (Richmond, Va., 1936), p. 210; William Mills to Peggy Mills, March 30, 1781; Peggy Mills to William Mills, April 17, 1781; [Genealogy of] The Quarles and Mills Families, typescript in *Chandler Collection*. Dr. Charles Quarles, trained first as a physician, later gave up his lucrative practice and received ordination as a Baptist minister in 1854. He died at his home (Inglewood) in the Greenspring area on August 20, 1881.

[12] Again, there is a detailed listing of Leroy Chandler's children in: Children Born to Leroy Chandler and His Two Wives, Eloisa Riddick Copeland and Sarah Ann Quarles, typescript in *Chandler Collection*.

[13] C.Q. Chandler II, Genealogical Notes. Chandler indicated that this infor-

mation was supplied by his aunt, Florence Chandler Ferguson. No date was affixed.

[14] Hattie Quarles Wyatt to Mrs. W.B. Gibson, October 13, 1936.

[15] Again, the experiences of Leroy and Sarah were chronicled in: Sarah Ann Quarles Chandler, Diary of a Trip from Virginia to Missouri, 1836; and *Boonville (Missouri) Weekly Examiner*, January 25 to March 8, 1935. The description follows the diary.

[16] Ralph Dickinson, Comments on Sarah Ann Quarles Chandler's Diary, undated typescript in the *Chandler Collection*.

[17] W.L. Sims, Belmont: The Home of Doctor Charles Quarles Chandler, November 18, 1925, typescript in *Chandler Collection*.

[18] Chandler Scrapbook. Pictures of Belle Monte, liberally annotated, were taken by C.Q. Chandler in December of 1938.

[19] C.Q. Chandler II, Genealogical Notes.

[20] Kelly Chandler to C.Q. Chandler II, November 13, 1923.

[21] Kelly Chandler to C.Q. Chandler II, November 29, 1923; Algernon Chandler to Annie Aull, May 8, 1903; Obituary, Sarah Ann Chandler, October 26, 1865, typescript in *Chandler Collection*.

[22] Chandler Scrapbook. Pictures of Inglewood, taken by Chandler on December 1, 1938, are liberally annotated. See also, Harris, *History of Louisa County*, p. 210.

[23] *Catalogue of the Officers and Students* (Richmond, Va.: Hampden Sidney College, 1847), pp. 1, 6; Willam Peffer (Dean, School of Medicine, University of Pennsylvania) to C.Q. Chandler II, January 7, 1924; Kelly Chandler to C.Q. Chandler, August 18, 1924; Florence M. Ferguson to C.Q. Chandler, December, 1923.

[24] Florence M. Ferguson to C.Q. Chandler II, December, 1923.

[25] C.Q. Chandler, Sr., to John B. Clark, Jr., January 7, 1875; *Columbia (Missouri) Herald Statesman*, December 7, 1933; March 23, 1938.

[26] R.S. Duncan, *History of the Baptists in Missouri* (St. Louis, Mo.: Scammell and Co., 1883), p. 819; *Columbia (Missouri) Daily Tribune*, May 26 and August 11, 1924; *Columbia Missourian*, May 26 and August 9, 1924; *Boonville (Missouri) Weekly Advertiser*, November 15, 1924; *Kansas City Star*, October 19, 1926; John O'Hart, The Woods Family, typescript in *Chandler Collection*. Anderson Woods marriage to Elizabeth Harris united the Woods with another colonial family of Welsh origin which first settled in Louisa and Albermarle counties in Virginia and later removed to Madison County, Kentucky. Genealogy of the Harris Family of Madison County, Kentucky, typescript in *Chandler Collection*.

[27] Florence M. Ferguson to C.Q. Chandler II, July, 1920; E.W. Stephens, Address at the Centennial of the First Baptist Church of Columbia, Missouri, November 18, 1923; Family Record of James H. Woods and Martha Jane Stone; John O'Hart, History of the Woods Family in Great Britain and America (1899). Typescripts of the above are in the *Chandler Collection*.

[28] E.W. Stephens to C.Q. Chandler II, December 12, 1923; Kelly Chandler to C.Q. Chandler II, December 2, 1923.

[29] Mrs. H.J. Hammond to C.Q. Chandler II, July, 1920; E.W. Stephens to C.Q. Chandler II, December 12, 1923. Dr. William S. Woods endowed William Woods College in Fulton, Missouri.

[30] The plight of Dr. Chandler and his wife is taken from: Charles Quarles

Chandler II, Sketch of Life of C.Q. Chandler, Jr., autobiographical typescript in *Chandler Collection*.

    ³¹ E.W. Stephens to C.Q. Chandler II, December 12, 1923.

Chapter 2

    ¹ Charles Quarles Chandler II began a serious investigation into his ancestry sometime after 1920. He regretted that he had not started earlier because he found that too few members of his parents' families were then alive to give him information. "In the light of this experience," he recorded, "it occurs to me my own children would in later years be interested in some of the more important things in my life." The result was an autobiographical "Sketch of Life of C.Q. Chandler, Jr.," a seven page narrative which chronologically highlights the events in his life from approximately 1870 to 1920. Other than a few minor factual errors, such as occasional incorrect date or an improper spelling, his recollections are remarkably accurate and easily verifiable in existing documents of the period. Thus, the information contained in this chapter, unless otherwise footnoted, follows his autobiographical narrative. A typescript of the "Sketch" is in the *Chandler Collection*. See also: *New Franklin (Missouri) News*, May 20, 1932; *Elkhart (Kansas) News*, June 15, 1933.

    ² See, for example: *St. Louis Post Dispatch*, September 12, 1929; *Wichita Beacon*, September 22, 1929; C.Q. Chandler, The United Baptist Church of Jesus Christ in Rocheport, Missouri, unpublished manuscript, *Chandler Collection*; *Columbia Missourian*, August 18, 1929; March 23, 1938; *Columbia Herald-Statesman*, December 7, 1933.

    ³ *Missouri Statesman*, February 24, 1875; *Rocheport (Missouri) Enterprise*, February 10, 1875.

    ⁴ Student Exhibition of the Rocheport Academy, December 23, 1879, an original program in the *Chandler Collection*.

    ⁵ Again, as stated in footnote 1 above, the factual information in this chapter follows Chandler's autobiographical narrative and will not be referenced hereafter.

    ⁶ E.W. Stephens to C.Q. Chandler II, September 12, 1923; Mrs. H.J. (Mattie Lee Chandler) Hammond to C.Q. Chandler II, July, 1920; copies in *Chandler Collection*.

    ⁷ *Elk City Globe*, June 13, 1883; R.L. Polk, *Kansas State Gazeteer and Business Directory*, 1882-83 (Denver: R.L. Polk and Co., 1883), p. 343; R.L. Polk, *Kansas State Gazeteer and Business Directory, 1886-87* (Denver: R.L. Polk and Co., 1887), p. 285.

    ⁸ *Elk City Globe*, June 13, 1883; April 3, 1884.

    ⁹ *Columbia (Missouri) Daily Tribune*, June 22, 1928.

    ¹⁰ *Barber County Index*, December 5, 1888; January 9, 1889.

    ¹¹ *Barber County Index*, July 10, 1889; *Medicine Lodge Cresset*, July 11, 1889; *Elk City Eagle*, July 12, 1889.

    ¹² *Barber County Index*, September 24, 1890; *Sioux City (Iowa) Journal*, July 12, 1933.

    ¹³ *Barber County Index*, March 9, 1894.

    ¹⁴ Genealogy of the Thayer Family; Reminiscences of Mrs. Emily F. Thayer; A Concise Copy of the Benedict Genealogy; typescript copies of all in *Chandler Collection*. Emily Thayer at age 85 visited Wichita in June of 1929 and recalled

in a news story the wagon trip she made from Illinois to Kansas in 1866. She had made the trip from Kansas City to Wichita aboard a Western Air Express Fokker tri-motor airplane. See the article, "Came to Kansas in Covered Wagon But Rides Planes Now," in the *Wichita Eagle*, June 18, 1929.

[15] *Medicine Lodge Cresset*, June 18, 1898; *Iola Register*, June 22, 1898; *Lincoln (Nebraska) Post*, June 22, 1898; *Barber County Index*, June 30, 1898. The marriage license, signed by Reverend H.O. Rowlands, Pastor of the Lincoln Baptist Church, and witnessed by numerous friends and relatives, is in the *Chandler Collection*.

[16] *Barber County Index*, May 2, 1898; December 3, 1898.

[17] Daisy Marita Bishop, Charles Quarles Chandler, II, September 17, 1939, unpublished manuscript in the *Chandler Collection*; *Barber County Index*, May 2, 1898.

[18] *Barber County Index*, undated news clipping in Chandler Scrapbook; Bishop, Charles Quarles Chandler, II, September 17, 1939.

[19] Memorandum of Agreement Between Geo. Theis, Jr., of Asland, Kansas, and J.W. Berryman and C.Q. Chandler, August 19, 1899, original handwritten document in *Chandler Collection*. See also, *Clark County (Kansas) Clipper*, July 18, 1935.

[20] Harry E. Chrisman, *Lost Trails of the Cimarron* (Denver: Sage Books, 1961), pp. 151-152.

[21] *Medicine Lodge Cresset*, June 7, 1899.

[22] *Medicine Lodge Cresset*, May 11, 1900; *Barber County Index*, September 20, 1901. To supervise the installation of the telephones, Chandler and Chase imported from Chicago a Mr. George Ball, "the man who made these phones." By September 18 he had installed 20 units. *Barber County Index*, September 18, 1901.

[23] *Medicine Lodge Cresset*, May 11, 1900.

[24] Elsberry Martin, The Purchase of the Kansas National Bank, October 24, 1938, unpublished manuscript in the *Chandler Collection*.

[25] H. Craig Miner, *A Short History of the First National Bank in Wichita, 1876-1976* (Wichita, Kan.: First National Bank, 1976), p. 7.

[26] *Medicine Lodge Cresset*, May 11, 1900.

[27] *Barber County Index*, undated news clipping, Chandler Scrapbook.

[28] *Barber County Index*, April 2, 1902. Waldron Chase was with C.Q. when he ordered and purchased the "gasoline motor wagon"in Wichita. Upon its arrival ten days later, the *Index* reported: "It is a dandy—an Olds—equipped with the latest gasoline motive power." See the *Barber County Index*, March 14, 28, 1902.

[29] *Barber County Index*, May 7, 1902; *Wichita Eagle*, undated news clipping, Chandler Scrapbook.

[30] *Barber County Index*, September 12, 1902.

[31] *Barber County Index*, September 9, 10, 1902; Condensed Report, Kansas National Bank, Wichita, Kansas, April 26, 1900, copy in *Chandler Collection*.

[32] *Barber County Index*, October 18, 1905.

Chapter 3

[1] H. Craig Miner, *A Short History of the First National Bank in Wichita, 1876-1976* (Wichita, KS: First National Bank, 1976), p. 7. This published version is

a summary of a longer study (also entitled, "A Short History...") which was written in observance of the Bank's centennial celebration.

² Chandler, Sketch of Life of C.Q. Chandler, Jr., *Chandler Collection.*

³ Chandler Genealogy, *Chandler Collection.*

⁴ *Barber County Index*, July 29, 1908; Chandler, Sketch of Life of C.Q. Chandler, Jr.

⁵ Interview, Anderson Chandler with author, May, 1982, *CEL Collection.*

⁶ Interview, Mrs. Alice Chandler with author, February, 1982, *CEL Collection.*

⁷ Church Calendar, First Baptist Church of Wichita, February 11, 1906; March 8, 11, 1906; June 7, 1906; January 15, 1911; October 14, 1914; February 4, 1925; Janauary 15, 1930; May 12, 1931. See also, C.Q. Chandler's Connection with the First Baptist Church, Wichita, unpublished manuscript in *Chandler Collection.*

⁸ *Kansas City Times*, July 9, 1925; *Kansas City Star*, August 18, 1934.

⁹ C.Q. Chandler II, Orthopoedic Work, unpublished manuscript, *Chandler Collection*; *Washington (Kansas) Register*, October 11, 1935.

¹⁰ *Kansas City Star*, August 18, 1934; Mr. and Mrs. C.W. Carter to C.Q. Chandler II, March 14, 1921, *Chandler Collection.*

¹¹ *Kansas City Star*, August 16, 1928; C.Q. Chandler II, Brief History, Crippled Children's Work, unpublished manuscript, *Chandler Collection.*

¹² *Wichita Eagle*, August 17, 1928; Chandler, Orthopoedic Work.

¹³ *Kansas City Star*, August 18, 1934.

¹⁴ *Wichita Beacon*, May 20, 1925; November 24, 1925; *Wichita Eagle*, May 20, 1925; *Kansas City Star*, July 9, 1925.

¹⁵ *Wichita Eagle*, August 17, 1928; *Kansas City Star*, August 18, 1934.

¹⁶ *Kansas City Star*, August 18, 1934.

¹⁷ *Topeka Daily Capital*, August 5, 1929; October 3, 1930; *Topeka State Journal*, October 2, 1930; *Neodesha Daily Sun*, August 13, 1930; *Wichita Beacon*, May 14, 1930; December 5, 1930; February 9, 1931; *Fort Scott Tribune*, December 5, 1930; *Lindsborg Progress*, January 15, 1931; *Pittsburg Headlight*, December 31, 1930; *Chanute Tribune*, Deember 18, 1930; *Lyons News*, January 9, 1931; *Iola Register*, January 5, 1931; *Hiawatha World*, January 2, 1931; *Abilene Reflector*, January 8, 1931; *Kansas City Times*, February 7, 1931; *Wichita Sunday Eagle*, February 22, 1931; *Clay Center Dispatch*, June 15, 1934; *Scott City Chronicle*, August 30, 1934.

¹⁸ *Barber County Index*, August 4, 1915.

¹⁹ *Wichita Beacon*, August 3, 1915; *Wichita Eagle*, August 4, 1915.

²⁰ *Wichita Eagle*, August 4, 6, 1915.

²¹ *Wichita Beacon*, August 3, 1915.

²² *Wichita Eagle*, August 4, 1915.

²³ *Ibid.*

²⁴ Chandler, Sketch of Life of C.Q. Chandler, Jr.

²⁵ Interview, Olive Chandler Clift with author, July, 1982, *CEL Collection.*

²⁶ Chandler, Sketch of Life of C.Q. Chandler, Jr.

²⁷ Reminiscences of George Throckmorton, unpublished manuscript, *Chandler Collection.*

²⁸ Interview, Olive Chandler Clift with author, July, 1982, *CEL Collection.*

²⁹ *Ibid.*; Chandler, Sketch of Life of C.Q. Chandler, Jr.

³⁰ The story of the summer vacation and subsequent marriage of C.Q. and

Alice was told by Olive Chandler Clift from her recollections of frequent discussions with her mother on the subject.

[31] Chandler, Sketch of Life of C.Q. Chandler, Jr.

[32] Interview, Olive Chandler Clift with author, July, 1982.

[33] Chandler, Sketch of Life of C.Q. Chandler, Jr.

[34] Interview, Olive Chandler Clift with author, July, 1982.

[35] Bulletin, First Baptist Church of Wichita, June 30, 1939; *Wichita Morning Eagle*, May 19, 1941; *Wichita Evening Eagle*, May 22, 23, 1941.

[36] *Wichita Eagle*, August 14, 16, 17, 1928; August 28, 1937; August 18, 1939; *Kansas City Star*, August 16, 1928; *Bank News*, May 15, 1931; *Wichita Beacon*, September 24, 1932; June 2, 1939; January 28, 1940; *Topeka State Journal*, February 16, 21, 1939.

[37] Chandler Genealogy, *Chandler Collection*.

[38] Interview, Olive Chandler Clift with author, July, 1982.

Chapter 4

[1] Miner, *A Short History of the First National Bank*, p. 6. Professor Miner's excellent study traces the growth of the FNB from its earliest predecessor in 1876—the Farmer's and Merchant's Bank—through the Bank's centennial year in 1976. Much of the factual information contained in this chapter, unless otherwise documented, has been liberally, and it is hoped accurately, restated from his work.

[2] C.Q. Chandler, Banks in Which I Have Been Interested, Both Financially and Responsible for the Management, unpublished manuscript, *Chandler Collection*. See also, *Wichita Eagle*, December 7, 1939.

[3] Interview, Paul Woods with author, February, 1982, *CEL Collection*.

[4] Daisy M. Bishop, Charles Quarles Chandler II, September 17, 1939, unpublished manuscript in *Chandler Collection*.

[5] *Wichita Beacon*, December 3, 1937.

[6] Bishop, Charles Quarles Chandler II, p. 6.

[7] Miner, *A Short History of the First National Bank*, pp. 6ff.

[8] A cashier's check in the amount of twenty five cents, executed during the Panic of 1907, is in the *Chandler Collection*. See also, R.M. Long, *Wichita Century: A Pictorial History of Wichita, Kansas, 1870 1970* (Wichita: Wichita Historical Museum Association, 1969), p. 124.

[9] O.H. Bentley (ed.), *History of Wichita and Sedgwick County, Kansas*, 2 vols. (Chicago: C.F. Cooper and Co., 1910), I, pp. 96-97. Naftzger was president of the Fourth National Bank in Wichita from 1893 until 1911. James H. Thomas, *A History of the Fourth National Bank and Trust Company* (Oklahoma City: Western Heritage Books, 1980), p. 15.

[10] *The Democrat*, October 22, 1932. For an excellent article on Chandler's philosophy on growth, see *Wichita Eagle*, June 13, 1933.

[11] *Wichita Beacon*, December 24, 1828.

[12] Frank Overton Carr, unpublished manuscript, *Chandler Collection*; *Wichita Beacon*, December 3, 1937.

[13] History of Frank L. Carson, unpublished manuscript, *Chandler Collection*; *Wichita Eagle*, Janauary 12, 1944; *Wichita Beacon*, January 12, 1944.

[14] *Wichita Beacon*, December 3, 1937.

[15] *Wichita Evening Eagle*, March 1, 1921.

[16] Miner, *A Short History of the First National Bank*, pp. 2ff.

[17] *Wichita Beacon*, December 33, 1937.

[18] Miner, *A Short History of the First National Bank*, pp. 8-9.

[19] *Wichita Evening Eagle*, March 1, 1921; *Wichita Eagle*, March 15, 1922.

[20] Interview, Dale Critser with author, May, 1982; Thomas, *A History of the Fourth National Bank*, p. 36.

[21] C.Q. Chandler to Henry J. Allen, September 21, 1921; Henry Allen to C.Q. Chandler, October 6, 1921; *Wichita Beacon*, December 24, 1928.

[22] J.W. McIntosh to C.Q. Chandler, August 30, 1926; February 18, 1927; April 26, 1927. C.Q. Chandler to J.W. McIntosh, September 27, 1926; February 3, 1927; April 26, 1927. Henry J. Allen to C.Q. Chandler, April 2, 1927. *Wichita Beacon*, December 30, 1928.

[23] *History of the Red Star Milling Company* (Wichita: Red Star Milling Co., 1921), pp.1-5; L.R. Hurd, To Whom It May Concern: Company Report, June 30, 1915; *Wichita Beacon*, March 22, 1930; "Early-Day Milling in Kansas," *The Northwestern Miller*, December 29, 1943; C.Q. Chandler, Red Star Mill and Elevator Company, unpublished manuscript, *Chandler Collection*.

[24] C.Q. Chandler, Red Star Milling Company, unpublished manuscript, *Chandler Collection*.

[25] *Wichita Beacon*, June 24, 25, 1928.

[26] C.Q. Chandler, What I Did with the Profit on Red Star Mill Company Stock, unpublished manuscript, *Chandler Collection*.

[27] C.Q. Chandler, Connection with Northwestern Mutual Life Insurance Company, Milwaukee, Wisconsin, unpublished manuscript, *Chandler Collection*; H.R. Ricker to C.Q. Chandler, August 6, 1928; *Wichita Beacon*, October 12, 1937.

[28] W.D. Van Dyke to C.Q. Chandler, January 26, 1928; March 16, 27, 1928; July 18, 1928.

[29] *Wichita Beacon*, July 23, 1928; December 24, 1928; C.Q. Chandler to Joseph Chapman, *et.al.*, September 14, 1932; C.Q. Chandler to L.J. Petit, October 12, 1932; *Milwaukee Sentinel*, October 20, 1932.

[30] C.Q. Chandler, [Special Meeting, Northwestern Mutual Life Insurance Company, October 18, 1932], unpublished manuscript, *Chandler Collection*.

[31] C.Q. Chandler, Panic—1933, unpublished manuscript, *Chandler Collection*.

[32] *Wichita Beacon*, December 3, 1937.

[33] C.Q. Chandler to W.D. Van Dyke, October 29, 1927.

[34] *Topeka Daily Capital*, February 13, 1935.

[35] Interview, Paul Woods with author, February, 1982.

[36] *Wichita Evening Eagle*, November 25, 1937.

[37] *Wichita Beacon*, October 4, 1936; J.J. Thomas to C.Q. Chandler, March 3, 1938; *Kansas City Times*, April 1, 1938; *Wichita Eagle*, April 1, 1938; *Wichita Beacon*, April 1, 4, 1938; *Denver Post*, July 24, 1938.

[38] C.Q. Chandler to C.J. Chandler, October 4, 1924; Alice Chandler to C.J. Chandler, October 7, ll, 23, 1924; November 8, 1924; *New York Times*, November 27, 1924. *Kansas City Times*, January 5, 1929; *Wichita Eagle*, January 20, 1929; March 23, 31, 1929; *Wichita Beacon*, January 24, 1929; February 11, 1929; March 26, 1929; April 14, 1929; July 21, 1936; September 5, 1936.

[39] *Wichita Evening Eagle*, December 12, 1938; February 15, 1939; April 18,

1939; May 6, 1939; July 10, 1939; September, 24, 26, 30, 1939; November 13, 14, 15, 1940; *Cherokee (Oklahoma) Republican*, July 4, 1941.

[40] *Boonville (Missouri) Advertiser*, January 25, 1935; February 1, 8, 15, 1935; March 3, 1935; C.Q. Chandler, Dear Grandmother, unpublished letters dated November 30, 1938, and December 1, 2, 3, 1938, *Chandler Collection*; *Wichita Eagle*, December 18, 1938.

[41] *Wichita Eagle*, June 6, 7, 1938; September 22, 1940; *Wichita Evening Eagle*, May 27, 28, 29, 30, 1940; July 3, 4, 5, 6, 8, 9, 10, 1940; C.Q. Chandler, Log of a Trip to Seattle, Washington, August 31 to September 18, 1940, unpublished manuscript, *Chandler Collection*; C.Q. Chandler, Automobile Trip to the Mississippi Delta, November 21-28, 1940, unpublished manuscript, *Chandler Collection*. The Delta trip was described by Victor Murdock in the *Wichita Evening Eagle*, December 2, 3, 4, 5, 6, 7, 1940.

[42] *Wichita Evening Eagle*, June 13, 14, 16, 17, 18, 19, 20, 21, 1941; November 18, 19, 20, 21, 22, 24, 25, 1941; *Houston Post*, November 15, 1941; C.Q. Chandler, Journey to Carlsbad Caverns, New Mexico, September 1-6, 1941, unpublished manuscript, *Chandler Collection*.

[43] *Wichita Beacon*, December 17, 18, 19, 1943.

[44] *Kansas City Star*, December 20, 1943; *Lyons (Kansas) News*, December 20, 1943; *Wichita Eagle*, December 20, 22, 1943; *Wichita Evening Eagle*, December 20, 21, 1943.

[45] *Wichita Beacon*, December 21, 1943.

[46] *Topeka State Journal*, December 21, 1943.

Chapter 5

[1] C.Q. Chandler II, Dear Grandmother, November 30, 1938, *Chandler Collection*; *Wichita Evening Eagle*, December 30, 1943.

[2] *Wichita Eagle*, December 30, 1943; *Wichita Evening Eagle*, December 30, 1943; *Burlington (Kansas) Republican*, January 21, 1944.

[3] Interview, C.Q. Chandler III with author, May, 1982, *CEL Collection*.

[4] Interviews, C.Q. Chandler III, George Chandler, and Paul Woods with author, February-May, 1982, *CEL Collection*.

[5] *Barber County Index*, undated newsclipping, *Chandler Collection*.

[6] *Wichita Eagle*, November 17, 1936; interviews, Paul Woods and C.Q. Chandler III with author, February-May, 1982, *CEL Collection*.

[7] *Wichita Eagle*, April 17, 1925.

[8] *Wichita Beacon*, July 25, 1928; January 13, 1944; *Wichita Eagle*, January 12, 1944.

[9] The biographical sketch of Charles Jerome Chandler's early life was obtained in a taped interview with Mrs. Alice Cromwell Chandler on March 6, 1982. Copy in *CEL Collection*.

[10] Charles Jerome Chandler left in the *Chandler Collection* a resume detailing the major events and professional accomplishments in his life covering the years 1902-1933.

[11] Interview, Alice Cromwell Chandler with author, March, 1982.

[12] *Gage (Oklahoma) Record*, August 8, 1924; *Wichita Beacon*, August 8, 1924; April 28, 1925.

[13] *Wichita Eagle*, April 13, 1925; *Wichita Beacon*, April 13, 1925.

[14] Interview, Alice Cromwell Chandler with author, March, 1982.

[15] Charles Jerome Chandler, Resume, *Chandler Collection*.

[16] Interview, Alice Cromwell Chandler with author, March, 1982.

[17] *Wichita Beacon*, July 25, 1928.

[18] *Wichita Beacon*, March 3, 1928; April 2, 1945; *Wichita Eagle*, July 2, 1945.

[19] Interviews, Alice Cromwell Chandler and C.Q. Chandler III with author, March-May, 1982, *CEL Collection*.

[20] Interviews, Gordon Evans, Alice Cromwell Chandler, and C.Q. Chandler III with author, March-May, 1982, *CEL Collection*. The first meeting of the group was in 1949. C.J. started the activity because he felt "that real silence is something nearly unknown to most of us, for when we are alone we turn on the radio or TV, or pick up a magazine or book. To me," he concluded, "it is very helpful to sit in silence with a group and have this type of fellowship." The format used was simple. Men entered in silence without greeting each other, and ten minutes of absolute silence were observed at the beginning and end of the 30 minute sessions. Devotional messages, delivered by one of the participants, were strictly limited to the middle ten minutes. See a more complete discription in *The Presbyterian Outlook*, May 6, 1958. A copy of the article, along with C.J. Chandler's "Memo to File, May 18, 1958," may be found in the *Chandler Collection*.

[21] Interviews, Gordon Evans and C.Q. Chandler III with author, March-May, 1982, *CEL Collection*.

[22] *Wichita Eagle*, February 22, 1933; October 28, 1933; May 15, 1940; *Wichita Beacon*, January 22, 1934; *Bank News*, May 15, 1935; *Round and Round* (Wichita Rotary Club), Vol. 25, No. 22 (November 28, 1941), pp. 1, 3.

[23] *Wichita Evening Eagle*, February 24, 1944; *Wichita Beacon*, December 27, 1944; February 21, 1945.

[24] *Wichita Eagle*, May 14, 1945; *Wichita Beacon*, July 7, 1945.

[25] Interview, Gordon Evans with author, March, 1982, *CEL Collection*.

[26] Miner, *History of the First National Bank*, pp. 45ff. Again, many of the facts relating to post World War II policy changes of the FNB are drawn from Miner's centennial history of the bank. See also, *Wichita Beacon*, June 2, 1951.

[27] Interview, Paul Woods with author, February, 1982.

[28] *Wichita Beacon*, September 10, 1952; *Wichita Evening Eagle*, August 10, 1953.

[29] *Wichita Eagle*, July 11, 1956; August 23, 1957; *Wichita Evening Eagle*, May 26, 1958.

[30] *Wichita Eagle*, June 11, 1958.

[31] Chrisman, *Lost Trails of the Cimarron*, pp. 151-152; The Woods Family in America, unpublished genealogy, *Chandler Collection*; *Wichita Beacon*, December 5, 1968; interview, Paul Woods with author, February, 1982.

[32] *Wichita Evening Eagle*, March 22, 1938; *Wichita Beacon*, December 5, 1968; interview, Paul Woods with author, February, 1982.

[33] *Wichita Eagle*, June 11, 1958.

[34] Miner, *History of the First National Bank*, pp. 57-59.

[35] Interviews, Paul Woods and C.Q. Chandler III with author, February, 1982; January, 1983, *CEL Collection*; C.Q. Chandler to author, January 25, 1983.

[36] Miner, *History of the First National Bank*, pp. 59-60.

[37] *Wichita Eagle*, July 14, 1971; December 16, 1974.

[38] *Wichita Eagle*, December 16, 1974.

[39] Interview, Gordon Evans with author, March, 1982.

[40] *Ibid.*

[41] Interview, Paul Woods with author, February, 1982.

[42] Interviews, Alice Cromwell Chandler, C.Q. Chandler III, and Jerome Chandler with author, March-June, 1982, *CEL Collection.*

Chapter 6

[1] Interview, George Throckmorton Chandler with author, April-May, 1982, *CEL Collection.*

[2] Interviews, Elizabeth Chandler Clogston, Olive Chandler Clift, George Throckmorton Chandler, and Anderson Woods Chandler with author, April-September, 1982, *CEL Collection.*

[3] C.Q. Chandler II, "Kansas Cares for Its Crippled Children," *The National County Magazine*, April, 1935, pp. 11, 29; C.Q. Chandler, Radio Address on Kansas Crippled Children, unpublished manuscript, *Chandler Collection*; *Manhattan (Kansas) Mercury*, March 11, 1935; *Topeka Daily Capital*, February 13, 1935; *Washington (Kansas) Register*, October 11, 1935; *Kansas City Times*, December 13, 1939; *Wichita Evening Eagle*, December 13, 1939.

[4] Interview, Elizabeth Chandler Clogston with author, September, 1982, *CEL Collection.*

[5] *Topeka Daily Capital*, February 13, 1935.

[6] Interview, Elizabeth Chandler Clogston with author, September, 1982; George Chandler (comp.), The Chandler Family, 1637-1978, unpublished genealogy, *Chandler Collection*; *Wichita Eagle⟨*, April 7, 17, 25, 1935; *Wichita Beacon*, April 7, 8, 17, 25, 1935.

[7] *Cherokee (Oklahoma) Messenger*, January 17, 1939; *Wichita Beacon*, January 16, 17, 1939; interview, Elizabeth Chandler Clogston with author, September, 1982.

[8] Interviews, George Throckmorton Chandler, Elizabeth Chandler Clogston, and Charles Quarles Chandler III with author, February-September, 1982, *CEL Collection.*

[9] *Ibid.*; *Wichita Beacon*, July 25, 1928.

[10] *Wichita Beacon*, July 25, 1928.

[11] *Holly (Colorado) Chiefton*, June 13, 1929.

[12] *Holly (Colorado) Chiefton*, September 19, 1929; November 25, 1930.

[13] George Chandler, The Chandler Family, 1637-1978; *Lyons (Kansas) Daily News*, March 9, 1934; *Wichita Eagle*, March 9, 1934.

[14] *Lyons (Kansas) Daily News*, March 9, 12, 1934; *Wichita Beacon*, March 9, 1934; *Bank News*, March 15, 1934, p. 4.

[15] Interview, Olive Chandler Clift with author, July, 1982, *CEL Collection.*

[16] Interview, George Throckmorton Chandler with author, April-May, 1982, *CEL Collection.*

[17] Interview, Charles Quarles Chandler III with author, February-May, 1982, *CEL Collection.*

[18] George Chandler, The Chandler Family, 1637-1978; interviews, Anderson Woods Chandler and Charles Quarles Chandler III with author, February-May, 1982, *CEL Collection.*

[19] Interview, Elizabeth Chandler Clogston with author, September, 1982.

[20] *Wichita Eagle*, October 28, 1928; *Wichita Beacon*, October 28, 1928.

[21] George Chandler, The Chandler Family, 1637-1978; interview, Elizabeth Chandler Clogston with author, September, 1982.

[22] *Ottawa (Kansas) Herald*, May 1, 1936.

[23] *Ibid.*

[24] George Chandler, The Chandler Family, 1637-1978; interview, Elizabeth Chandler Clogston with author, September, 1982.

[25] Interview, Elizabeth Chandler Clogston with author, September, 1982.

[26] *Wichita Eagle*, July 8, 1938.

Chapter 7

[1] Much of the information in this chapter has been obtained from personal interviews with those whose biographies are summarized hereafter. Most of the facts and details on Olive Chandler Clift's life, unless otherwise cited, are drawn from a lengthy, recorded interview with her on July 6, 1982, at the home of Charles Quarles Chandler III in Wichita, Kansas. The audiotapes are in the *CEL Collection*.

[2] Interviews, George Throckmorton Chandler, Anderson Woods Chandler, and Elizabeth Chandler Clogston with author, April-September, 1982, *CEL Collection*.

[3] *Wichita Eagle*, January 5, 6, 1938; interview, Anderson Woods Chandler with author, May, 1982, *CEL Collection*.

[4] *Wichita Eagle*, January 17, 1937.

[5] *Wichita Beacon*, September 11, 1937; *Wichita Eagle*, September 11, 1937.

[6] Interview, Anderson Woods Chandler with author, May, 1982; *Wichita Eagle*, January 5, 6, 1938.

[7] Interview, Alice Cromwell Chandler with author, March, 1982, *CEL Collection*.

[8] Interviews, George Throckmorton Chandler, Anderson Woods Chandler, Charles Quarles Chandler III, and Jerome Lewis Chandler with author, April-July, 1982, *CEL Collection*.

[9] The facts and information which follow on the life of George Throckmorton Chandler, unless otherwise cited, were obtained in lengthy, recorded interviews with him on April 5, April 21, and May 12, 1982, in Wichita, Kansas, the audiotapes of which are in the *CEL Collection*.

[10] Interview, Olive Chandler Clift with author, July, 1982.

[11] *Wichita Beacon*, July 21, 1936; November 15, 1936. George kept a diary of his experiences, a part of which was reprinted in the *Wichita Sunday Eagle*, September 5, 1936.

[12] *Wichita Beacon*, July 24, 1942; November 15, 1942; *Wichita Eagle*, September 7, 1942.

[13] *Wichita Evening Eagle*, March 13, 1943; *Wichita Beacon*, August 3, 1943; November 11, 27, 1943; *Wichita Eagle*, November 11, 12, 27, 1943; December 21, 1943; January 10, 1944.

[14] *Wichita Beacon*, March 16, 1944.

[15] *Wichita Eagle*, December 5, 1945.

[16] Here again, the continuity of George Throckmorton Chandler's biographical sketch follows the information recorded by the author during interviews with him in April and May of 1982, the audiotapes of which are in the *CEL Collection*.

[17] "Bob Chandler ... Part of a First Tradition," *Newsletter: First National Bank of Pratt*, Vol.1, No. 3 (September-October, 1982), p. 4; George Throckmorton Chandler to author, September 8, 1982.

[18] The major portion of the biographical data which follows on Anderson Woods Chandler was recorded in a lengthy interview with him on May 19, 1982, in Wichita, Kansas, and is on file in the *CEL Collection*.

[19] Interview, Olive Chandler Clift with author, July, 1982.

[20] Interview, George Throckmorton Chandler with author, April-May, 1982.

[21] Interview, Olive Chandler Clift with author, July, 1982.

[22] One record of his activities at Robinson Junior High School may be found in the *Wichita Beacon*, November 40, 1940.

[23] Here again, the facts which follow on Anderson Woods Chandler are consistent with the information obtained from the interview with him on May 19, 1982, the audiotapes of which are in the *CEL Collection*.

[24] Interview, George Throckmorton Chandler with author, April-May, 1982.

[25] Interviews, George Throckmorton Chandler, Charles Quarles Chandler III, and Jerome Lewis Chandler with author, April-July, 1982.

[26] *Wichita Eagle*, January 4, 1961.

Chapter 8

[1] The Chandler Family, 1637-1978, *Chandler Collection*.

[2] Interview, Alice Cromwell Chandler with author, March, 1982, *CEL Collection*.

[3] The biographical facts presented in this chapter, unless specifically and otherwise documented, were obtained during lengthy interviews with Charles Quarles Chandler III on February 16, 1982, and May 17, 25, 27, 1982. The data have been liberally enriched also by information obtained in interviews with Mrs. Alice Cromwell Chandler, his mother, and Georgia Johnson Chandler, his wife. Audiotapes of the interviews are in the *CEL Collection*.

[4] *Wichita Beacon*, June 24, 1951.

[5] *Wichita Beacon*, January 10, 1951.

[6] The Chandler Family, 1637-1978, *Chandler Collection*; interview, Georgia Johnson Chandler with author, December, 1982, *CEL Collection*.

[7] *Topeka Daily Capital*, January 6, 1956.

[8] *Wichita Eagle*, June 11, 1958.

[9] *Wichita Eagle*, April 28, 1959.

[10] *Wichita Eagle*, August 23, 1957; *Wichita Evening Eagle*, May 26, 1958.

[11] Interviews, Paul Woods and Charles Quarles Chandler III with author, February-May, 1982, *CEL Collection*.

[12] *Wichita Eagle and Beacon*, June 7, 1980.

[13] See the Annual Reports for 1965 and 1970 published by the First National Bank in Wichita; see also, *Wichita Eagle*, July 14, 1971; December 16, 1974; *Wichita Beacon*, September 30, 1971; March 21, 1975.

[14] *Wichita Beacon*, September 30, 1971.

[15] *Wichita Beacon*, August 1, 1973; October 17, 1973; *Wichita Eagle and Beacon*, March 2, 1975.

[16] See the *Annual Reports* published by the First National Bank in Wichita for each of the years cited.

[17] *Wichita Eagle and Beacon*, March 2, 1975.

[18] *Wichita Eagle and Beacon*, June 7, 1980.

[19] See the *Annual Report for 1981* published by the First National Bank in Wichita.

[20] First National Bank in Wichita, *Condensed Statement of Condition*, December 31, 1982.

[21] *Notice of Special Meeting of Stockholders To Be Held November 18, 1982* (Wichita, Ks.: First National Bank in Wichita, 1982), pp. 10-12. This elaborate document, a feasibility study dated October 15, 1982, was prepared by the Board of Directors of FNB for consideration by their stockholders' at a special meeting on November 18, 1982. It was distributed over the signature of C.Q. Chandler III, Chairman of the Board. The purpose and objectives of the planned reorganization are found on pp. 7-9.

[22] *Wichita Eagle and Beacon*, November 27, 1982.

[23] *Ibid.*

[24] Interviews, George Throckmorton Chandler, C.Q. Chandler III, and Georgia Johnson Chandler, April, 1982-January, 1983, *CEL Collection;* George Chandler, The Chandler Family, 1637-1978, *Chandler Collection.*

[25] Most of the information relating to the personal history of Chuck's family was provided by Mrs. C.Q. (Georgia) Chandler III during lengthy interviews at her home on January 12 and 24, 1983, audiotaped copies of which are in the *CEL Collection.*

[26] Interview, C.Q. Chandler III with author, January 24, 1983, *CEL Collection.*

[27] C.Q. Chandler III, Unpublished Resume, *Chandler Collection.* The discussion which follows, detailing Chandler's business and civic involvements, is drawn from this document.

[28] *Kansas Society for Crippled Children* (Wichita, Ks.: Kansas Society for Crippled Children, 1973), pp. 1-3; interview, C.Q. Chandler III with author, January 24, 1983.

[29] Interview, C.Q. Chandler III with author, January 24, 1983.

Chapter 9

[1] *Wichita Eagle and Beacon*, March 2, 1975.

[2] The biographical data for Jerome Chandler were obtained during a lengthy interview session in his office at the Farmers State Bank in Sterling, Kansas, on Sunday, June 6, 1982. Copies of the audiotapes of the interview are in the *CEL Collection.*

[3] Interview, Charles Quarles Chandler III with author, May, 1982, *CEL Collection.*

[4] The biographical data for Charles Quarles Chandler IV were obtained during a lengthy interview in his office at the First National Bank in Wichita on Thursday, December 2, 1982. Audiotaped copies of the interview are in the *CEL Collection.*

[5] Interview, Gordon Evans with author, March, 1982, *CEL Collection.*

[6] The author, as an ex-officio member of the Wichita Chamber board, was privileged to share the goodwill mission to London with Mr. Chandler.

[7] Interview, Charles Quarles Chandler III with author, May, 1982, *CEL Collection.*

[8] The genealogies, which are entitled "The Chandler Family," are in the *Chandler Collection*; copies are in the author's possession.

[9] George Throckmorton Chandler, History of the Hymer Pasture, *Chandler*

Collection; interviews, George Throckmorton Chandler, Anderson Woods Chandler, Elizabeth Chandler Clogston, Olive Chandler Clift, and C.Q. Chandler III with author, April, 1982-January, 1983, *CEL Collection*.

[10] William Bannowsky to author, September, 1979.

BIBLIOGRAPHY

A. THE CHANDLER COLLECTION:

The Chandler Collection had its origin in the second decade of the twentieth century when Charles Quarles Chandler II gave the first organization to a spate of materials which he had inherited and otherwise loosely collected. Impressed by what he found and desiring to learn more about his ancestry, he spent a decade of hard research and amassed an impressive amount of genealogical materials which confirmed the richness of his heritage. That vast, well organized collection contains diaries, autobiographical notes, genealogies, letters, newspaper clippings, professional journal entries, books, memorabilia, and photographs, a good portion of which relates to his own personal and professional activities from 1883 to 1943. Those wishing to examine the materials will find them in the possession of his grandson, Charles Quarles Chandler III.

B. THE CENTER FOR ENTREPRENEURSHIP LIBRARY COLLECTION:

The Center for Entrepreneurship and Small Business Management at Wichita State University maintains significant holdings on subjects relating to the starting and managing of small businesses. The Collection consists of books, periodicals, journals, newspaper files, statistical treatises, and other empirical research data. An important section of the CEL Collection includes audio and video tapes by and/or about entrepreneurs who began small and grew large in the private business sector. The following audiotaped interviews, relating to the lives and experiences of the Chandlers of Kansas (1883-1983), are now a part of those library holdings:

Chandler, Alice Cromwell, with author, March 6, 1982
Chandler, Anderson Woods, with author, May 19, 1982
Chandler, Charles Quarles III, with author, February 16, 1982; May 17, 25, 27, 1982; January 24, 1983
Chandler, Charles Quarles IV, with author, December 2, 1982
Chandler, George Throckmorton with author, April 5, 21, 1982; May 12, 1982
Chandler, Georgia Johnson, with author, January 12, 24, 1983
Chandler, Jerome, with author, June 5, 1982
Clift, Olive Chandler, with author, July 6, 1982
Clogston, Elizabeth Chandler, with author, September 28, 1982
Critzer, Dale, with author, May 25, 1982
Evans, Gordon, with author, March 24, 1982
Woods, Paul, with author, February 22, 1982

C. UNPUBLISHED MATERIALS:

Bishop, Daisy, Charles Quarles Chandler II. September 17, 1939.

241

Carr, Frank Overton. Unpublished Resume. [n.d.].
Carson, Frank L. Unpublished Resume. [n.d.].
Chandler, Charles Jerome. Unpublished Resume. [n.d.].
Chandler, Charles Quarles II. Automobile Trip to the Mississippi Delta. November 21-28, 1940.
——————————. Brief History, Crippled Children's Work. [n.d.].
——————————. Children Born to Leroy Chandler and His Two Wives, Eloisa Reddick Copeland and Sarah Ann Quarles. [n.d.].
——————————. Connection with the First Baptist Church, Wichita. [n.d.].
——————————. Connection with the Northwestern Mutual Life Insurance Company, Milwaukee, Wisconsin. [n.d.].
——————————. For My Children. [n.d.].
——————————. Genealogical Notes. [n.d.].
——————————. Journey to Carlsbad Caverns, New Mexico. September 1-6, 1941.
——————————. Log of a Trip to Seattle, Washington. August 31 to September 18, 1940.
——————————. Orthopoedic Work. [n.d.].
——————————. Panic — 1933. [n.d.].
——————————. Radio Address on Kansas Crippled Children. 1934.
——————————. Red Star Mill and Elevator Company. [n.d.].
——————————. Red Star Milling Company. [n.d.].
——————————. Sketch of Life of C.Q. Chandler, Jr. [n.d.].
——————————. [Special Meeting, Northwestern Mutual Life Insurance Company, Milwaukee, Wisconsin. October 18, 1932.
——————————. What I Did with the Profit on Red Star Mill Company Stock. 1930.
Chandler, Charles Quarles III. Unpublished Resume. [n.d.]
Chandler Genealogy. [n.d.].
Chandler, George Throckmorton. The Chandler Family, 1637-1966.
——————————. The Chandler Family, 1637-1978.
——————————. The Chandler Family, 1637-1982.
——————————. History of the Hymer Pasture. 1983.
Chandler, Sarah Ann Quarles. Diary of a Trip to Missouri. 1836.
——————————. Last Will and Testament. October 25, 1859.
Chandler, William W. Last Will and Testament. May 20, 1779.
Church Calendar. First Baptist Church of Wichita. 1906, 1911, 1914, 1925, 1931.
Concise Copy of the Benedict Genealogy. [n.d.].
Dickinson, Ralph. Comments on Sarah Ann Quarles Chandler's Diary. [n.d.].
Family Record of James H. Woods and Martha Jane Stone [n.d.].
Ferguson, Mrs. Florence M. Account of My Family. [n.d.].
Genealogy of the Chandler Family. [n.d.].
[Genealogy of] Charles Quarles Chandler II. [n.d.].
[Genealogy of] The Quarles and Mills Families. [n.d.].
Genealogy of the Thayer Family. [n.d.].
Lineage of Richard Chandler, 1577-1632. [n.d.].
Martin, Elsberry. The Purchase of the Kansas National Bank. October 24, 1938.

Memorandum of Agreement Between Geo. Theis, Jr., of Ashland, Kansas, and
   J.W. Berryman and C.Q. Chandler. August 19, 1899.
Missouri [Society for Crippled Children] Extends Congratulations. 1934.
Obituary. Sarah Ann Chandler. October 26, 1865.
O'Hart, John. History of the Woods Family in Great Britain and America. 1899.
   ——————. The Woods Family. [n.d.].
Reminiscenses of Mrs. Emily F. Thayer. [n.d.].
Reminiscenses of George Throckmorton. [n.d.].
Skaggs, Jimmy M. Wichita, Kansas: Economic Origins of Metropolitan Devel-
   opment. 1978.
Sims, W.L. Belmont: The Home of Doctor Charles Quarles Chandler. Novem-
   ber 18, 1925.
Stephens, E.W. Address at the Centennial of the First Baptist Church of Co-
   lumbus, Missouri. November 18, 1923.
Wood, Arthur L. Unpublished Resume. [n.d.].

D. NEWSPAPERS:

Abilene (Kansas) Reflector, 1931
Barber County (Kansas) Index, 1888-1915
Boonville (Missouri) Weekly Advertiser, 1924, 1935
Burlington (Kansas) Republican, 1944
Chanute (Kansas) Tribune, 1930
Cherokee (Oklahoma) Messenger, 1939
Cherokee (Oklahoma) Republican, 1941
Clark County (Kansas) Clipper, 1935
Clay Center (Kansas) Dispatch, 1934
Columbia (Missouri) Daily Tribune, 1924, 1928
Columbia (Missouri) Herald Statesman, 1933, 1938
Columbian Missourian, 1924
Democrat (Wichita, Kansas), 1932
Denver (Colorado) Post, 1938
Elk City (Kansas) Eagle, 1889
Elk City (Kansas) Globe, 1883
Elkhart (Kansas) News, 1933
Fort Scott (Kansas) Tribune, 1930
Gage (Oklahoma) Record, 1924
Hiawatha (Kansas) World, 1931
Holly (Colorado) Chiefton, 1929, 1930
Houston (Texas) Post, 1941
Iola (Kansas) Register, 1898, 1931
Kansas City Star, 1925, 1926, 1928, 1934, 1943
Kansas City Times, 1925, 1929, 1931, 1935, 1938
Lincoln (Nebraska) Post, 1898
Lindsborg (Kansas) Progress, 1931
Lyons (Kansas) News, 1931, 1934, 1943
Manhattan (Kansas) Mercury, 1935
Medicine Lodge (Kansas) Cresset, 1889, 1898, 1899, 1900
Milwaukee (Wisconsin) Sentinel, 1932
Missouri Statesman, 1875

New Franklin (Missouri) News, 1932
New York Times, 1924
Ottawa (Kansas) Herald, 1936
Pittsburg (Kansas) Headlight, 1931
Pueblo (Colorado) Star-Journal, 1934
Rocheport (Missouri) Enterprise, 1875
St. Louis Post Dispatch, 1929
Scott City (Kansas) Chronicle, 1934
Sioux City (Iowa) Journal, 1933
Topeka (Kansas) Daily Capital, 1929, 1935, 1956
Topeka (Kansas) State Journal, 1930, 1939, 1943
Washington (Kansas) Register, 1935
Wichita (Kansas) Beacon, 1915, 1924-1980
Wichita (Kansas) Eagle, 1915, 1925-1981
Wichita (Kansas) Eagle and Beacon, 1975, 1980-1982
Wichita (Kansas) Evening Eagle, 1921, 1936, 1938-1941, 1943-1945, 1953, 1958

E. PUBLISHED MATERIALS:

Abbot, Jack. "A Wichita Man Makes Time His Pet Hobby," *Wichita Eagle Sunday Magazine*, June 13, 1926, p. 3.

Annual Reports. Wichita, Ks.: First National Bank in Wichita, 1945-1981.

Bentley, O.H. (ed.). *History of Wichita and Sedgwick County, Kansas* 2 vols. Chicago: C.F. Cooper and Co., 1910.

Bulletin. Wichita, Ks.: First Baptist Church of Wichita, 1939.

Catalogue of the Officers and Students. Richmond, Va.: Hampden-Sidney College, 1847.

Chandler, Charles Jerome. "World Security: A Personal Matter," in Wallace C. Speers (ed), *Laymen Speaking*. New York: Association Press, 1947, pp. 167-175.

Chandler, Charles Quarles II. "Kansas Cares For Its Crippled Children," *National County Magazine*, April, 1935, pp. 11, 29.

————————. "Six Thousand Crippled Children in Kansas," *Elliott's Monthly*, March, 1931, p. 10.

Chandler, George Throckmorton. "Bob Chandler ... Part of a First Tradition," *Newsletter: First National Bank of Pratt*, Vol. 1, No. 3 (September-October, 1982), p. 4.

["Charles Jerome Chandler"], *Round and Round: Wichita Rotary Club*, Vol. 25, No. 22 (November 28, 1941), p. 1.

Chrisman, Harry E. *Lost Trails of the Cimarron*. Denver: Sage Books, 1961.

Condensed Report. Wichita, Ks.: Kansas National Bank, 1900.

Duncan, R.S. *History of the Baptists in Missouri*. St. Louis: Scammell and Co., 1883. "Early-Day Milling in Kansas," *The Northwestern Miller*, December 29, 1943.

Edwards, Harry Stillwell. *Eneas Africanus*. Macon, Ga.: J.W. Burke Co., 1951.

Harris, Malcolm H. *History of Louisa County, Virginia*. Richmond, Va., 1936.

History of the Red Star Milling Company. Wichita, Ks.: Red Star Mill and Elevator Company, 1921.

Hurd, L.R. *Company Report*. Wichita, Ks.: Red Star Mill and Elevator Company, 1915.

Kansas Society for Crippled Children. Wichita, Ks.: Kansas Society for Crippled Children, 1973.

Kansas State Gazeteer and Business Directory, 1882-83. Denver: R.L. Polk and Co., 1883.

Kansas State Gazetter and Business Directory, 1886-87. Denver: R.L. Polk and Co., 1887.

Kyne, Peter B. *The Go-Getter: The Story That Tells You How To Be One.* New York: Holt, Rinehart and Winston, 1949.

Long, R.M. *Wichita Century: A Pictorial History of Wichita, Kansas, 1870-1970.* Wichita, Ks.: Wichita Historical Museum Association, 1969.

"Michael J. Cleary—President," *Field Notes [Northwestern Mutual Life Insurance Company]*, Vol. 32, No.3 (November, 1932), p. 2.

Miller, Glen W., and Jimmy M. Skaggs. *Metropolitan Wichita: Past, Present and Future.* Lawrence: Regents Press of Kansas, 1978.

Miner, H. Craig. *A Short History of the First National Bank in Wichita, 1876-1976.* Wichita, Ks.: First National Bank in Wichita, 1976.

The Name and Family of Chandler: Genealogy and Historical Sketch. Washington, D.C.: Media Research Bureau, 1924.

Notice of Special Meeting of Stockholders To Be Held on November 18, 1982. Wichita, Ks.: First National Bank in Wichita, 1982.

Reed, John. "Wichita Contributes to the Memory of a Statesman," *Wichita Eagle Sunday Magazine*, March 13, 1927, p. 3.

Reed, William H. "Bankers I Have Known," *Bank News*, May 15, 1931, p. 2.

Thomas, James H. *A History of the Fourth National Bank and Trust Company.* Oklahoma City: Western Heritage Books, 1980.

Wigfield, Marshall. *History of Caroline County, Virginia.* Richmond, Va.: Trevvet Christian and Co., Inc., 1924.

Wood, L. Curtise. *Dynamics of Faith: Wichita, 1870-1897.* Wichita, Ks.: Center for Management Development, 1969.

Zurnow, William Frank. *Kansas: History of the Jayhawk State.* Norman, Okla.: University of Oklahoma Press, 1957.

INDEX

247